Pond'rings

a writer's memoir

Marcia Lee Laycock

Published by Siretona Creative. www.siretona.com

978-1-998249-37-4 Electronic book
978-1-998249-36-7 Paperback

Cover photo of pond by Marcia Lee Laycock
Cover photo of author by Meagan Pyra
Cover and interior design by Colleen McCubbin

Text typeset in Kings Caslon Display

Printed in Canada by Blitzprint, Calgary

Distributed to the trade by Ingram Book Company.

Endorsements

What my friend Marcia writes, I read. She's down home, real deep, and fun in a funny sorta way. You'll want a dozen copies of *Pond'rings*. Give it to friends and watch the ripple effects.

Phil Callaway
Canadian Author

Pond'rings is more than a memoir. It is a coming-to-life story built on courageous honesty and told with the artistry Marcia Laycock is known for. Be prepared: as you read it, you will find yourself coming to life as well.

Nancy Rue
author, mentor, podcaster

Pond'rings follows a life of growth into belonging and belief, both in oneself and in One who is beyond us, wrapped up in the sometimes mystifying calling to write. Marcia Laycock's honesty, resilience and willingness to change will inspire you, even if you are not a writer.

Sigmund Brouwer
Canadian author

Marcia Lee Laycock has shared her refreshingly candid and delightful personal story about being a writer of faith. She takes us from the wilds of the Yukon to the deep waters of the Great Lakes. It's a gentle triumphant memoir about endurance, passion, and the discipline of continually retuning one's ear to God's call. It celebrates all efforts to follow one's dreams, and also affirms doing small things with great love.

Lucia Frangione
author of the novel, *Grazie*

In her signature style of raw honesty and transparency, Marcia invites us into the tapestry of her journey, woven with divine encounters and "God-incidences." Through the pages of this memoir, she paints a picture of courage and faith that led her to her calling as a writer. As I read, I found a spark to reignite my own creative path. If your soul seeks inspiration and your heart craves upliftment, this book will be a treasured companion.

Kimberley Payne
author of the *Meeting Faith* devotional series

Reading Marcia Laycock's book, *Pond'rings*, feels a bit like a roller coaster ride. Which is just what the Christian life can feel like! Her story will make you smile, cry a little, gasp in amazement, and often praise God for how He works in a believer's life. Life with God is certainly not boring. What I loved best about Marcia's story is her authenticity. I often said to myself, "Yep," as I read, because many of her responses to God echo my own.

Pam Halter
children's book author and editor

"Write your own people," said Rudy Wiebe at a Canadian Writers' Conference where I first met author Marcia Laycock. In *Pond'rings*, a truly fine memoir, Marcia has done just that. With authenticity, vulnerability and humor, she takes us on her faith journey to inform and inspire as she shares her people with us. An enriching, grace-filled story of God's timing and faithfulness.

Jane Kirkpatrick,
award-winning author of
Across the Crying Sands

Could anything good ever come of a frightened young girl who found solace in writing while curled up in a tight cubby hole? Yet it was here that Marcia Laycock found the quiet and privacy she needed to express her creativity and discover her love of writing, which would fuel a lifelong passion.

Pond'rings is a profound, captivating memoir. A skilled word-crafter, Marcia quickly draws the reader into her life story, stirring imagination and emotions, leaving the reader wanting more.

Marcia chronicles the long bumpy road of finding confidence as a writer while navigating self-doubt, rejection, and discouragement. Yet, despite these challenges, Marcia draws attention to the "God interventions," which in time became clear, giving her the will to persevere.

The frightened young girl of the past is today a respected and honored writer, globally. Readers around the world have benefitted from her writings and applaud her relatability and heart of integrity and truth.

Pond'rings belongs in your hands! You too will benefit from the deep spiritual well of Marcia Laycock.

Margaret Gibb
Founder *&* Executive Director
Women Together

Dedication

This book is dedicated to all writers of faith, those whose careers have spanned decades and those who are just beginning. May you be encouraged to persevere, to hold to the course God has laid out for you, acknowledge Him and praise Him for who He is and what He has done in your life and through your work.

Table of Contents

Introduction: Daughter of Shallum

I stumbled upon Nehemiah 3 some time ago and it stopped me in my tracks. I love this book in the Old Testament because it reveals God's commitment to preserve His people, His Word, and His reputation on this earth. The third chapter is a long list of all the men who worked on repairing the walls of Jerusalem. We are told their names and the portion of the wall they worked on. In the middle of the list of men verse 12 reads, "Shallum, the son of Hallohesh, ruler of half the district of Jerusalem, repaired, he and his daughters"(ESV).

The daughters are not named, but I think they must have had some kind of stature among the people and those doing the work to have been mentioned at all. I was thrilled to find them there. These were women who moved outside of what would have been considered "normal" in their day and age. They did not do what was expected of them. They chose a different path, one that they likely were ridiculed for. They may have had to endure the disapproving looks and whispers behind hands.

I am familiar with that concept. Being a writer in a small rural church lends itself to the same. I am encouraged by these women who did what God called them to do. As a writer of faith I follow in their footsteps. I too am all about building the walls that will guard God's reputation and bring glory to His name on this earth. It is what I am called to do, the path upon which God has led me from a very young age.

You are about to read a number of stories about me, but please know that this is not just my story. This is God's Story, a journey He laid out for me before I was conceived in my mother's womb. As David said in Psalm 139:13-16 (ESV):

> For you formed my inward parts;
> you knitted me together in my mother's womb.
> I praise you, for I am fearfully and wonderfully made.
> Wonderful are your works;
> my soul knows it very well.
> My frame was not hidden from you,
> when I was being made in secret,
> intricately woven in the depths of the earth.
> Your eyes saw my unformed substance;
> in your book were written, every one of them,
> the days that were formed for me,
> when as yet there was none of them.

And then there is Ephesians 2:10, which says, "We are his workmanship, created in Christ Jesus for good works which God prepared beforehand that we should walk in them" (ESV).

I believe that the work I do as a writer of faith is a major part of those "good works." They are threads spun and coloured by God and woven into a tapestry that is not only for my benefit but for the service and encouragement of others. It has been said that we are only looking at the underside of the tapestry He is creating, and yet I have seen the beauty and am amazed at the pattern, even though I have not yet seen the whole of it.

As believers in Christ, our primary calling is to love God with all our mind, heart, and strength, or as the old Westminster Catechism says, "to glorify God and enjoy Him forever." I love that phrasing because it tells me God wants me to have joy in Him, joy in the people around me, joy in the life and work He has given me to do.

Our secondary calling as Christian writers is to proclaim Christ, in all His glory, through the words, the stories, the plays, the poems He gives us. As we do that, He will take those words and move the hearts and souls of our readers closer to Him. Perhaps even for the very first time.

My journey as a Christian writer has proven that premise over and over again, in spite of my weaknesses and failings, in spite of my stubbornness and pride. He has worked miracles. Miracles! Through my words! He has also given me opportunities to teach and mentor younger writers. What an incredibly humbling thing to realize. When I remember that fact, all the struggles and frustrations are worth it. Lives are being changed in the building of the kingdom of God on this earth and He has graciously given me a part in it, as He did with the daughters of Shallum.

Soli Deo Gloria

Chapter 1

The little girl clapped her hands over her ears to try and keep out the harsh voices coming from the rooms below. She picked up a pencil and the notebook her mother had bought her and opened the small door into the little room her father had fixed up under the eaves in her bedroom. He called it her "cubby hole." She pulled on the cord that turned on the bare lightbulb, arranged her dolls around a small chair, and wrote them a story.

That little girl was me.

Our home was rather stressful, mostly because of my mentally ill grandmother, my mom's mother, who had come to stay with us after the apartment building in which she lived burned down.

Grandma had been sent out to work in a large house near Buckingham Palace when she was just eleven years old. She was not treated well there, and my mother speculated that at some point in her young life Grandma was raped. Understandably, she hated men.

When she found herself pregnant as the First World War ended, she sailed to Canada with her two-month-old daughter and married the man who had impregnated her. The marriage was short-lived. She drove her new husband away and became a single mother, doing whatever she had to do to survive. Over time she became an angry, bitter woman.

Grandma hated my father, which caused a lot of grief for everyone in the household. Though it became apparent that she was mentally ill, it was the era when such things were never discussed. A diagnosis was never sought. My parents just dealt with the situation as best they could.

Looking back on that time, I know I used writing as a way to escape the harsh words and constant bickering that filled the days and nights. I could most often be found in that little cubby hole under the eaves in my bedroom, writing poems and short stories for my dolls. They didn't complain so I kept doing it. Even at that young age, writing became an obsession. I remember the day it became a necessity.

I am standing at the top of the wooden staircase, holding onto the banister, running my palm along its smooth surface—the surface polished by my grandmother's hands. It smells of beeswax.

I clutch the side of my flared skirt, the one Grandma remade from one of my older sister's castoffs. Grandma had worked at it in her room, late at night, her frustrated murmurings making me giggle as she tried to make the ancient sewing machine work, though I knew the words she muttered were forbidden ones. The hum of the machine put me to sleep there, in her room, night after night, but I always woke in my own bed.

I had worn that skirt almost every day since the day Grandma disappeared.

I take a step down, listening to a man's deep voice at the door. Another step, another, and I see him: a tall man in a policeman's uniform. He's holding my grandmother's coat—the thin blue one she had been wearing, a feeble effort against the cold of that last November day. My mother had begged her to accept a new one she'd bought for her that week. I shiver, remembering the cold look I saw in Grandma's eyes

16

that day when she raised her chin and shook her head, clutching the scarf at her throat. "I don't feel the cold," she said.

I sit on a stair, twist the cloth of the skirt in my hands, lean forward to hear the policeman's words.

"We found it near the tail race," he was saying—the part of the dam that carries water away from the flooded locks where freighters and ocean-going vessels are lifted and allowed passage. And I saw the water in my mind, water spilling over the barriers at the locks where the freighters pass between the two great lakes, Huron and Superior. I saw the water and the white froth and shivered again. How cold it would have been.

I remembered she had said her father once told her that drowning was a pleasant way to die. At some point Grandma's mental anguish overcame her desire to live. I imagined her slipping into the silken green swirl, the weightlessness a final letting go. Then I thought, *Why did she take her coat off?* I knew it wouldn't have mattered if she had worn it. The churning water would have taken her down in minutes.

I see the stiffness of my mother's body, see her hands shake as she reaches for the coat. She speaks so softly I can't hear her words. The policeman says something about being sorry and something about sending someone to identify the body.

The body. My grandmother. I slip down onto the next step and it creaks. My mother looks up at me. There are no tears in her eyes yet, just the sorrow. A sorrow deeper than any I'd ever seen before.

"Come down," she says.

I stand and somehow put one foot in front of the other, descending as though in slow motion, the burning knot in my stomach telling me I have done something terribly wrong. *It was me. I made Grandma want to die.* I want to scream the words, but they lodge in my throat, a jagged stone threatening to stop my breath. She hugs

17

me and I feel her breath go in and out. She pats my shoulder and goes to the phone. "I'll have to call your father," she says, but just holds the receiver in her hand and stares out the window for a long time before dialing the number.

"Come home," I hear her say. "The police were just here."

He comes and they leave together. When they come back my mother rushes to the bathroom. I hear her vomiting. Then it's quiet. But she doesn't come out right away. I go upstairs and stand at the top again, waiting for her. I hear my father on the phone, saying the body wasn't identifiable. "Been in the water too long," he says, "but we knew the dress and her ring. Yes, we're sure."

I hear my mother crying then, alone in the bathroom.

I wanted to go to the funeral, but my mother's reasoning seemed right. "You kids are too young. No need for you to see ..."

"I'll babysit." My sister's words came quickly. I felt her urgency to help, but I also knew it was a way to avoid going with them. Twelve years my senior, she was old enough, but she, too, had been the brunt of Grandma's cruel ridicule too often.

"We'll be home before you know it," my dad said as they left.

I wondered what they did, what they said there. Did they hold hands or lean into one another? Did my mother cry? Did my father? Did they feel guilty about being relieved of Grandma? As I did.

The phone calls started that day. My sister answered once, told my father someone had said, "How do you feel now?"

"What did they mean, Dad?" she asked.

My father shook his head. "Never mind. Don't answer the phone anymore. Leave it to me."

I overheard my mother telling a friend that Grandma had spread lies about my father throughout the neighbourhood. I saw him answer several times and slam the receiver down. He would go outside then and sit on the back step and smoke his pipe. I watched from the window, the gray puffs chuffing hard into the air.

Some of the neighbours brought food. I liked that. Eating was good to do when things weren't going right. I learned that early, from Grandma, who always smiled when I asked for more, so I always did, even if it was tuna casserole. Food was supposed to make it all better. Food and a cup of tea. But not even our next-door neighbour's delicious lasagna could do that now.

It was my brother who first said the words to me. "Grandma's dead."

I slapped him. My mother put her hand on my arm. But she said nothing. Silence had become the new rule. My brother followed me into my room and said it again. I raised my fist but did not strike.

"I know," I said. "You don't have to say it."

His shoulders sagged. "Okay." He turned away but stopped at the door. "Want to go play in the fort?"

I shrugged but there was something pleading in his eyes. I followed him. The fort was a cave in a pile of boulders in the back alley, just big enough for the two of us. My brother had hung a piece of ragged blanket over the entrance, held in place by a board held down by stones. A semblance of privacy to hide us from the world and all our imagined enemies.

We sat in silence for a time, the dampness of the hard earth clinging like wet cloth. I tinkered with the plastic tea set Grandma had given me for Christmas the year before, but didn't pretend to make tea.

"Do you think she's in heaven?" my brother asked.

I wrinkled my brow. "That's a stupid question. Stupid. Stupid." The harsh words hovered between us.

I crawled out of the dim dank place and ran down the alley, swiping at the tears. I couldn't stop them now. Because Grandma couldn't be in heaven. I'd heard the priest say so, the one who came to talk about where they could bury her, where they could not bury her.

Because Grandma never went to church. I ran there, to the imposing building surrounded by a black wrought-iron fence, its cross-topped spire thrusting up into a somber sky. I picked up a stick and ran it along the fence, around and around the manicured grounds until a thought made me stop. *What if God is sleeping? What if I wake him up? He'll be mad at me.*

I flung the stick between the bars of the fence onto the lawn. "I don't care!" I screamed the words again. And again. "I don't care! I don't care!"

I wanted to ask my father where they had buried her. I started to once, but his eyes flashed to my mother's face, and he shook his head before I could finish the question. That's when I learned not to speak, not to argue, not to disrupt the disturbing quiet that had settled on our home. The source of disruption was gone now. It would be a sin to bring it back again.

The only thing I could do now was crawl into my cubbyhole and write.

Chapter 2

During that time when I struggled with the grief over my grandmother's death, I often went to my room, sat on my bed, and wrote a few lines in the small green diary my mother had given me. I'd never written much in it previously, never written about anything present tense, anything real, but during that time I needed to pour out the confusion, the anger, the pain, the guilt. The first entry was brief. *Grandma is gone*, I wrote. *Grandma is gone*.

There was a Big Old Hairy Ogre—the BOHO—tormenting me, blaming me. He kept whispering in my ear that I was the reason Grandma had thrown herself into the tail race. I couldn't write that accusation. Somehow putting it in that small diary would make it true. Though I believed it was, I could not put it into words.

I continued to write in that small diary and in other journals I gathered along the way, as well as scribbling down the stories that often swirled around in my brain. My teachers at school encouraged me and, as encouragement will, that spurred me on to write more. Then, when I was eleven years old, an aunt and uncle came to visit. They brought a box of books. One of them was wrapped in bright paper.

"This one is for you," Aunt Ethel said. Her heavy perfume wafted around me, her dyed black hair and bright red lipstick reminding me what my mother had said about my aunt's attempts to make us all believe she wasn't really fifteen years older than my uncle Orm. He winked at me and nodded. I carefully unwrapped the package and ran my hand over the picture on the cover. A young girl with a blue bonnet and pink skirt, her hands clasped to her breast, her expression wistful. Emily of New Moon by Lucy Maude Montgomery.

I read it slowly, savouring the story about that young girl who actually called herself a writer. When I came to the end of it, I determined that someday that's what I would be. When I look back on it now, I believe that book was not just a random gift from my aunt and uncle, but a gift from God, a way for Him to set me on the path to be what He created me to be—a writer.

I kept writing and had the privilege of having some wonderful teachers. But my first English teacher in high school, an elderly nun named Sister Mary Immaculate, was not an encourager. In fact, she was one of the people who helped the BOHO's voice grow stronger. She was a tiny woman, with plump pink cheeks that seemed to want to burst out of the wimple of her veil, and round gold-rimmed glasses that perched low on a thin nose.

Like all the nuns at that school she did not abide any nonsense in her classroom and expected us to adhere strictly to the rules. I was used to that, having already come through eight years of parochial schooling, but this was high school, and I was particularly anxious to do well in Sister Mary's class. She wasted no time in assigning us to prove our worth as writers. I worked hard on my first short story and handed it in with no little amount of fear and trembling. Was it good enough? Would this teacher also praise and encourage me?

I was devastated and in tears when that paper came back with a large red F written across the top. The teacher's piercing blue eyes made me quiver when she took me aside at the end of the class.

"You have plagiarized and that is a sin!"

Tears slipped down my cheeks.

"Do you know what that word means?"

I gulped and shook my head. "No, Sister."

She explained it clearly, waving my assignment in my face. "Go home and tell your parents what you have done."

The BOHO screamed in my ear again, laughing at me for thinking my writing was worth being praised. It took me a while to get my sobs under control when I showed my mother the F-marked paper and told her what the teacher had said.

My mother calmed me down and asked if I still had copies of the other short stories I'd written in my last year of elementary school. When I brought them to her, she slipped them into a large manilla envelope with a note to Sister Mary.

My hands were shaking once again when I handed it to the teacher. She called me aside at the end of that class and told me she was going to change the mark she'd given my story to a B. She didn't apologize and I never managed to gain an A on any assignment that year. Neither did I ever get another F, but deep down the hurt lingered and fed the doubt that I could ever be a good enough writer, or, in fact, a good enough human being. Score—BOHO 1, Little Girl Writer 0.

Another of my high school teachers, Mrs. Burgess, was also known for demanding excellence from all her students. She always wore conservative clothing, often grey or black, and her white shirts looked as stiff as a nun's scapular. Her short auburn hair lay flat, her ruddy cheeks a contrast to the bags under her eyes. Everyone stepped aside when she strode down the hallways of Mount St. Joseph College. Sitting in her grade eleven class, I quickly realized that her formidable demeanour became irrelevant when she began to teach. I began to realize that there were skills to be learned in this writing game, and she was determined that I learn them and learn them well. I owe her a great debt to this day.

It was under Mrs. Burgess' supervision that my class published an anthology of short stories and poetry. I was pleased when she told me one of my poems would be published in it and I was especially thrilled when the title of that poem, Training Wheels, was chosen as the title for the booklet. It was spiral bound and printed on a mimeograph machine, but I could not have been prouder. I was a published writer! For a short time the score was even—Little Girl Writer 1, BOHO 1.

A short time before graduating from that high school, Mrs. Burgess stood before the class and leaned toward us. "I know some of you want to be writers." Her gaze fell on me and I held my breath.

"But I want you to remember something." She scanned the room. "If you don't have something of value and significance to say, don't you dare write."

It was another pivotal moment in my young writing life. I'm sure she would have been horrified to discover that her words had a negative effect on me. Although I had continued to receive a lot of praise for my writing in school, I did not believe I could possibly have anything of value to say to anyone, so, other than the assignments that had to be done for school, I stopped writing.

The root of this low self-esteem came from an incident that had occurred when I was about eight years old. I realize now it was the day on which the BOHO was conceived, a day that is curiously hazy in my memory.

I remember strolling down the long lane that passed the summer cottages and homes along the edge of Munuscong Bay on the north shore of Lake Huron. I was heading for the farm at the end of that lane, intending to play with the two girls who lived there, or perhaps help them with their chores. As I passed a small green cottage another girl stepped out of the

24

driveway. I stopped when she smiled. I had met her before but something about her kept me away.

She waved me over. "Want to play a game?" She seemed eager. I shrugged. "Okay."

She slipped her arm through mine and led me toward the cottage. The back door of the car parked in the drive stood open. She slipped inside and giggled at the man waiting there.

"You like playing cards?" he asked.

I shook my head. He shuffled the deck in his hand. "Hmmm. Okay, we could play something else." He slipped the cards into his pocket and opened the opposite door, waving us out behind him. "How about hide and seek? Lucy (*not her real name*) loves that game. Don't you?" He grinned at her. "We'll hide first. You count to ten, Lucy, then try to find us." He winked at her.

Lucy giggled again. The man's hand felt clammy when he took mine and led me into the bush. We hadn't gone very far when he squatted and pulled me closed beside him. "Let's lay down," he said, "so she won't see us."

I didn't know what to do when his hand slipped into my shorts. I lay still, staring into the green leaves above.

As I walked back home, the deep-seated belief that I had done something terribly wrong, which took root when my grandmother died, asserted itself once again. The traumatic incident coloured everything that happened in my life from then on. It became the pivot on which everything else turned and affected how I saw myself and my world.

I now believed I was a bad girl with a dark secret that could never be told. It even affected how I saw God. He had always seemed to be far away but now He was watching me, and He carried a big stick. BOHO 10, Little Girl 0.

I was raised in a home where God was given some acknowledgement. And God was mentioned quite a bit in the schools I went to, so I knew a lot about Him, and knew all the rules and regulations He supposedly expected me to adhere to, but I did not understand what it meant to have a relationship with him.

As I watched some of my teachers in that high school, I realized a few seemed to know God in a way that shone through their lives. I wanted to be like them, but the more I tried to do all the right things, the more frustrated I became. I knew I was just faking it. The BOHO told me I would never succeed and once again I believed his lies.

By the time I reached the end of high school I decided that God did not want anything to do with me. This of course was in line with my conviction that I was not acceptable, not good enough for Him. Because of that one dark incident that occurred when I was a child, I believed I could not be accepted or loved by anyone, most especially God. I believed I could not accomplish anything that was worthy of His approval or even His attention. I became filled with anger and bitterness and decided that if God wanted nothing to do with me that was just fine because I wanted nothing to do with Him. Chalk up another big one for the Big Old Hairy Ogre.

When I finished high school, I checked my bank account and decided I had enough saved up from working part time for the past four years, to give myself a graduation present. I wanted to see the Rocky Mountains so I booked a train trip to Banff, Alberta. When I researched what to do in Banff, I discovered the Banff School of Fine Arts had a summer creative writing program. I signed up for that too, knowing very little about the instructors but thinking it would broaden my horizons, so to speak.

The main instructor was Harry J. Boyle, who had a long list of journalism and broadcasting credits attached to his name. Mr. Boyle gave lectures on life and writing that were riveting and inspiring.

There was also a poetry teacher there and it was from him that I learned what constructive criticism looked like. When I handed in my first assignment, he was blunt. "This is not poetry," he said, "but it's well written." He then proceeded to introduce me, and the other students, to good poetry, and coached me on how to write using concrete imagery and internal rhyme and rhythm. They were skills I have been very grateful to have learned over the years.

The school also opened my mind and heart to the beauty of ballet, opera, and classical music, all performed on the stage and free to attend, since I was a student. I was exposed to some extremely talented young people from all across North America and beyond. One girl I met there became a life-long friend.

Another pivotal moment in my writing life came after I returned from Alberta, when it was time to decide which university to attend. I knew I wanted to write so I considered two schools—Carleton University in Ottawa, the number one school for journalism in the country at the time, and the University of British Columbia in Vancouver, which had one of the best creative writing programs.

My dad sat me down at the table in our small kitchen one day. It was a rare thing for him to make a point of entering into a conversation with me, so I leaned forward as he spoke.

"I know you want to write, and I think you have the talent to do it," he said, "but the reality is, you can't make a living writing short stories and poetry in this country. I think you should study to be a journalist."

It was a brief but significant conversation that dovetailed with my admiration for Harry Boyle and made me choose Carleton University. I think the fact that UBC was on the other side of the country may have had something to do with my father's advice, but I saw the wisdom in his words and followed them, though

I often have wondered how my life would have been different had I not.

I spent two years at Carleton, and for the most part I enjoyed the studies. I selected a double major for the first year, taking Journalism and Honours English. It was a good balance of studying English literature and learning the parameters and skills needed in the field of the Canadian press. I loved the studying and did well on my assignments and exams.

A highlight came unexpectedly at the end of the first term. I was packing my books into my backpack at the end of a creative writing class when the professor called out to get our attention. "Remember, your journals are due tomorrow."

I frowned and turned to the girl beside me. "Journal? What journal?" Her eyes widened. "Don't you remember? He told us at the beginning of the term that we were to write a daily journal. It will be a big chunk of our final mark!" I'm sure my heart skipped at least one beat. I must have been absent the day that assignment was given out.

I stopped by the bookstore on my way home, bought a journal with a plain cover and spent the next twenty-four hours writing and post-dating all my "daily" entries. When it was handed back to me, the note on the last page of that journal made me give a big sigh of relief. "You write well. Come to my office for a chat."

I remember that meeting clearly. I sat on the edge of a straight-backed wooden chair and trembled as the professor told me he thought I had a bright future as a writer. His words thrilled me, but later when I contemplated what he'd said, the ogre started whispering in my ear again. "That teacher must have an ulterior motive. He just praised you to lure you into some kind of illicit relationship."

I decided to ignore any further invitations to chat.

As that first year at Carleton came to a close, I had another decision to make. I was not allowed to continue studying in both majors, so I had to choose between the two. It was about that time when I had what I believe was a divine appointment, in an elevator, as I was on my way to a class. One of my English Literature professors stepped into the elevator beside me.

"Have you decided which major you'll choose?" she asked.

I shook my head. "No, but I'm leaning toward Journalism."

The professor huffed. "Well, that's a waste of good talent!"

I huffed back. How dare she not believe I was a good enough writer to become a journalist. *I'll show you!* I thought.

Looking back on it now, I realize I should have been thrilled at the compliment she'd given me, but, again, no doubt because of that deep-seated belief that I was not worthy, I received her words from a negative perspective. I've never been much of a planner, but at that point I set my feet on the path to be a journalist without thinking at all about what that might look like.

Chapter 3

I'm one of those writers who doesn't lay out the plot or outline the story before I begin to write. I rarely begin at the beginning since the story comes to me in scenes. That means it usually takes a lot of re-working to organize the story so that it makes sense. I do eventually make a timeline of sorts, once I get into it, but that's about it. I love the excitement of not knowing where I'm going.

Both in writing and in life, this can have some interesting consequences. Many times, I've ended up in places I would never have even thought about, let alone planned for. When a friend at Carleton told me she was going to Spain with her geology class, I was envious. Then she said, "They've just opened up more seats for anyone who wants to go. You should join us." Another friend said we could travel together, so I borrowed some money from my brother, got a part-time job on campus, and signed up.

It was a trip full of the unexpected. One day my friend and I found ourselves sitting by a fountain in the middle of Lisbon, Portugal, looking at a map. A young man approached and asked what we were looking for. We knew he was one of the gigolos we'd been watching from the balcony in our hostel, but I told him we wanted to go to the Castle of San Jorge. He offered to take us there.

It wasn't until we found ourselves in the oldest part of Lisbon that I realized perhaps we should have thought more carefully before saying yes. It was only when looking back at that time that I realized what a risk we had taken. And I thank the Lord for His protection. Perhaps I should have remembered an old Irish proverb, "Trust God but don't dance in a small boat!"

That experience ended up being fashioned into a poem:

Sanctuaries

I am leaning on the fountain:
pack on my back,
jeans, Tshirt, running shoes.
He is watching, by the fountain
water flowing out of marble
a cold grey stone, waiting to pick
the one he wants. He wants the one in
middle age, well dressed, in high heels
clicking on the tiles, the deep blue Moorish tiles
of Lisbon, Portugal.

I watch him as he finds her, follows
at a distance, the enticing flow
of dress and yellow hair, then
meets her on the corner, tells
his eyes to smile, speaks to her
in Spanish, Portuguese, knowing
she will shake her head, then finally
in English, tells her
there is a restaurant nearby,
watches for the snap around her eyes
that tells him she doesn't care anymore,
but sees instead the crinkle of a laugh that says
she's flattered, but ...
he flips a hand in mock salute, saunters
back toward the fountain where

I am staring at the castle on the hill,
map spread, the wheel of Lisbon whirling
and he asks, "Where is it you want to go?"

I lift my chin and nod to "the Castle.
The Castle of San Jorge."
"There is a bus,"he says, "or ...
I could take you there."

I watch his eyes.
He grins. "No charge today."
I drop my eyes. He shrugs. Walks away.
I fold the map and follow.

He gives a guided tour, points out
the places tourists flock to see, then
stops, turns, faces me.
"Now we go around, or this way,"pointing
to a street of ancient stone. He
studies me.
"You could not go this way alone."
I nod and we proceed.
"Stay close,"he warns, then
suddenly
the sun is cut away
the day grown quickly cold
closed in by weeping walls. The way
is steep and smells of fish and
acrid smoke from charcoal stoves
set out by doorways choked with crouching
women ringed by thin and grimy
children crying, screaming at
chickens squawking running in all directions
and here and there a man
slouches and stares.

At last we find
escape, the hole of light ahead.

I force my eyes to see nothing but
the glare as we climb worn stone stairs and
step out quickly, quickly
I let go, amazed
I have been clutching at his shirt.
We stand together looking
down into the darkness, the sudden silence
then turn away and up through daylight where
the buses gleam and rumble and
tourists pour into the street.

We wander through the gardened castle
grounds manicured and combed while
peacocks strut and screech
tourists congregate to buy
ice cream and gaze at the wide
unbroken view.

He tells me it was built to be a palace
by the Moors until the Christians came
and conquered "but now
it is just a sanctuary
for the birds."

I lean against thick parapets
that hide with chill complicity
the blood of their own history
while he stares down toward the streets
where he was born, eyes flashing dark as
darkened stone and says,
"From here you cannot see ... only
the sun gleaming on the water."

Where ships lie precariously
thinking they are safe and sheltered
in the harbour.

I realize now that in life, as in writing, it is wise to be at least a little bit prudent in planning for the future. Yes, God will lead and direct and I should trust Him, but I should also realize that He gave me a mind with which to think, and plan. This doesn't mean that I should make plans and then ask God to bless them, but rather, I should open my mind, my eyes and my ears to see and hear what God might be planning for me. If I am attentive, I know I will discover that He is leading and guiding in all aspects of my life, confirming the direction in many ways.

I did not think about such things at the time, but that summer I believe God led me to take a job in a fishing lodge in northern Ontario. I worked with a crew of young people and loved swimming and boating on the beautiful Esnagi Lake during our off hours. The job paid reasonably well, and there was nowhere to spend my wages, so by the end of the summer I had enough money to head back to Carleton University, where I enrolled in the journalism program. I don't regret the choice. I learned some valuable writing skills that have served me well to this day. But by the time I finished the second year I realized that journalism was not a good fit for me. Much of the course at Carleton centred on politics, and I had no interest at all in going to Parliament Hill to interview those who were on the back benches at the time. Neither was I interested in covering the debates which often seemed like little more than tantrums you might see in a kindergarten. I began to realize I would never be good enough to succeed in that profession. I did not have the aggression needed, nor the desire to continue. I was also very lonely there. I missed the friends I had made at the fishing lodge.

Near the end of the second year, I received a letter from one of the young men I'd worked with in northern Ontario. The letter detailed how he and some of my other friends were building "a cabin in the wilderness" near Talkeetna, Alaska. My hands shook a bit when I read his next words. "Why don't you come and help? You'll like it here."

Since I liked him, it did not take me any time at all to decide that's what I wanted to do. I finished the term at Carleton, worked long enough to put some money in the bank, and ended up on a bus to Prince George, my first stop on the way to Alaska. After a short visit with my brother, I purchased an airline ticket to Anchorage, arriving there fairly late at night. I tried to contact my friends, but they did not respond so I purchased a map of the city, intending to take a taxi and find a youth hostel.

A few phone calls later it looked like I would have to spend the night in the airport. I was examining the map again when a young woman who was manning the car rental booth approached and asked what I was looking for. When I explained that I intended to stay in the airport she told me that would not be possible since it would be locked up at midnight. I asked if there was a hostel within walking distance. She cocked her head at me. "Do you realize that Anchorage has been designated the rape capital of North America right now?"

I shook my head. No. I did not know that. She invited me to stay the night with her. Seeing no alternative, I said yes, and continued to try and contact my friends. Two days later I decided to just get on the train and go find them. I knew I would have to get off the train at mile 222. It was a slow ride, during which a few, mostly First Nations people, got off and on. The steward tapped me on the shoulder as the train ground to a stop at mile 222. There was no platform of any kind, only a small wooden marker beside the tracks. I got off and looked around for some kind of trail. None to be found. I sat down on my pack and wondered how long it would take me to walk to Talkeetna, or for the train to return on its way back to Anchorage. Would I be spending the night alone in the Alaska wilderness?

Then I heard an odd sound. I cocked my head and heard it again. A cow? Out here in the middle of nowhere? Or was it a moose? The bellow came again and I decided it was definitely a cow. One of my friends had mentioned there was a small farm near where they were building the cabins. I followed the sound and came upon a log cabin surrounded by gardens and a few animals, including the bellowing cow. I knocked on the door and was greeted by a rather surprised farmer. He informed me that my friends had gone to Anchorage for the weekend. He said he knew where their cabin site was, sort of, and offered to take me there. After a long slog through muskeg swamp we found the three wall tents. The farmer said good-bye and I picked a tent to sleep in for the night. Two days later my friends arrived. I'm sure I was much more glad to see them than they were to see me.

I loved living in the bush but after a few weeks began to feel the stress of being a third wheel, so to speak. When my money began to run out as the end of the summer approached, I convinced one of the couples who had just gotten married to take me with them on their honeymoon. I promised I would part ways with them as soon as we crossed the border. They dropped me off in the Yukon, in a small town called Dawson City.

Dawson was bustling with young people, some there to work through the summer to make enough to go back to college, others looking for a "back-to-the land" lifestyle. It was that group that drew me in and convinced me to stay. As the days went by, I settled into the rhythm of life there.

It was the early 70s. The tumultuous 60s had calmed somewhat, though the rebellious climate was still being felt. The Vietnam War was raging, as were the protests, and many draft dodgers had made their way north. I was sitting in a bar with a couple of them, watching a news broadcast about the war. A village had just been hit by napalm. The camera zoomed in on a man carrying his dead child away from their burning home, then back out again to the face of the journalist whose voice, matter of fact and emotionless, detailed the number of dead, the reason for the bombing, and the overall advancement of the war.

Like my friends, I was disgusted. It seemed the story was all that mattered to that journalist. I wanted to scream, "Don't you see the man? Can't you see his agony?" That was the day I decided I had made the right decision not to become a journalist.

Since I had just spent two years at university studying to become just that, the moment was rather significant. It solidified my determination to separate myself from the prevailing culture. The world was a mess. Dawson seemed like a good place to try to find a way to survive it and perhaps keep the chaos at bay.

After spending about a year in Dawson, I decided it was time for a break. Another winter was on the horizon, and I wasn't sure how I would survive it in Dawson, so I packed up my vehicle and headed for Whitehorse. I found a small cabin to rent a few kilometers out of town and registered for an arts program at Yukon College.

The instructor was Ted Harrison, who was to become one of Canada's famous and well-loved landscape painters. He was a lovely man who had attracted an eclectic group of students to study everything art-related, from pottery and weaving to portrait sketching and painting. I could write a book about that group and about Ted himself, who was the consummate absent-minded professor. We all adored him.

I wasn't far into the program when I realized there were a few people there who were using art as therapy.

One was a young aboriginal boy who was incarcerated in the Whitehorse juvenile detention centre. Ted had arranged for him to be there because he recognized the boy's talent and wanted to encourage him. Sadly, that story did not end well. That young man became an alcoholic and eventually committed suicide.

Another was a former helicopter pilot who was in rehab, and an architect who had suffered a nervous breakdown while working for a huge company in Vancouver. His wife attended the class too, for moral support. She provided us all with quite a bit of entertainment. She was as large and loud as her husband was small and quiet. I got to know and like them both and often stayed overnight at their apartment through that winter, when the weather was too bad to make the drive home.

Eventually I got to the point, toward the end of the winter semester, when I trusted that woman enough to show her some of my poetry and short stories. Unbeknownst to me, she made copies of some of them and sent them to a professor in the creative writing department at the University of British Columbia, who happened to be a good friend. She walked into the classroom at Yukon College one day and handed me a large manilla envelope.

"What's this?" I asked.

"An application for the Creative Writing Program at UBC," she replied. "It's just a formality. You've already been accepted."

I was stunned. And, at first, thrilled. But as I thought about what moving all the way to Vancouver would mean, I hesitated. I knew UBC was a huge university in a huge city, in which I knew no one. I remembered the lonely days at Carleton and did not wish to repeat them. The BOHO was sneering at me. "You could never survive down there. That prof probably accepted you just because his friend asked him to. You'd be humiliated by all the others who really deserve to be there." I feared it was true and I began to wonder how such a drastic change would affect my life and my writing. Hadn't I come north to escape a culture of hypocrisy and deceit? I decided it would not be a good shift. The envelope remained unopened. I have often speculated as to how my life would have been different had I filled out that form and had the courage to go.

As the days lengthened, a bustling summer in Dawson began to appeal once again. When a friend offered me a job there, I packed my vehicle and headed north. And once again I found myself caught up in all the craziness of a northern town full of young people there to make money and party as much as possible.

It was during that summer in Dawson City that I met a young man who was to change my life. I looked out the window of my cabin one afternoon and saw him making his way up the path. He wore a fringed leather jacket and floppy leather hat. *Who on earth is this?* I wondered. I opened the door to his knock and found myself staring into the most startling blue eyes I thought I'd ever seen.

His name was Spencer and he was there to pick up some pottery equipment left there by a previous tenant who now lived in a cabin just below me. We chatted for a while and he continued on his way.

Though the memory of him lingered, I did not see him again for several weeks. I learned that he was one of a rather reclusive group of "hippies" living out in the bush about sixty kilometers from Dawson. It seemed our paths were not destined to cross until he showed up at my workplace one day and asked if I wanted to go have a picnic at North Fork, a branch of the Klondike River.

When one of my best friends, Pauline, discovered we had gone on a date she was thrilled. Spence had often helped her through a long cold winter when her husband was working away. "If I wasn't already married," she said, "I'd be going after that one." She made it her business to put us together whenever she could, but the Big Old Hairy Ogre was still active, telling me there was no way that young man would be at all interested in me.

It was at a July 1st celebration that I stopped listening and finally realized Pauline was right, and Spence and I began to spend time together. I was astonished to discover he wanted to be with me and seemed, perhaps, even to love me. Of course, the BOHO was screaming that it could not be true, but eventually I agreed to move in with Spence and pursued the "alternative" lifestyle practiced by many of our friends at the time. That consisted of partying a lot, working when we had to, and living for the moment. We rented a small cabin just out of town that first winter. (And here's a tip for you: if you ever live in the far north, do not spend the winter in a small cabin on the north side of a hill—it makes for a very long dark winter.)

It was during that time, while surviving temperatures that often dropped into the minus 60-degree Fahrenheit range, that I sat by my wood stove and wrote my first novel. It was a fantasy about talking ravens and, fortunately, it has never been published. I was also introduced to the work of Rudy Wiebe that winter. *The Temptations of Big Bear* instilled in me the power of setting and poetic language and pure sing-it-to-the-world story.

As the days and weeks went by, I was caught up in the story I was creating and realized, once again, that writing was still of supreme importance to me. It was my way of escape when I needed one, my way of dealing with the world. When I was lonely, I wrote. When someone hurt me, I wrote. On those rare occasions when I was happy, I wrote. I told myself that living, and sometimes barely surviving, one day at a time was the way to go. And I wrote.

I never showed any of my writing to anyone, because I did not believe I had value in anyone's eyes. I did not believe that anything I wrote could be of interest or significance to others. (The BOHO was still winning. Forgive me, Mrs. Burgess.)

It was a long cold winter during which "cabin fever" threatened more than once. But we got through it (the writing helped), and when the spring finally came, we leaped at an opportunity to purchase some titled land, a rare thing in the Yukon. We hauled an old trailer onto the property to live in and began building an eight-sided log house on the edge of a hay field on the banks of the Klondike River. The work was hard and moved rather slowly since we both had jobs in town during the week.

I was determined not to live in a dark cabin again, so insisted on peeling and bleaching the logs. There were moments when I despaired of ever seeing those logs set into walls, but with the help of friends who often dropped by to help, and the 24-hour daylight which allowed us to work well into the night, eventually we could see progress. It was a good way to keep myself too busy to think about the discontentment I still felt. And when I could grab a moment or two, I kept writing to escape it. Though I would not admit it, I was miserable. The writing was only a band aid, not a solution to the inner restlessness and unease that had always plagued me.

Chapter 4

By the end of October the days, and especially the nights, were getting cold. Our eight-sided log house was almost finished when my best friend's husband showed up one day with a gift for his wife—a St. Bernard puppy named Blossom. He asked if we would keep it for a couple of days so he could give it to her on her birthday. We put Blossom in the kennel we had beside the old trailer. Blossom did not like the kennel. We went to bed that night but could not sleep because of her whining and howling.

"I'm going to bring her in," Spence said.

I did not think that was such a good idea. "You know what puppies do, and if she does, I'm not cleaning it up."

Blossom settled down quickly once she was inside. But the next morning, when I stepped into a warm squishy pile of something that did not smell good, I poked Spence and repeated my words. "I'm not cleaning it up."

I went into the kitchen to make coffee and discovered there were several piles of puppy poop all over the floor of the trailer, most of them frozen, because the small wood stove had gone out in the night.

I felt a bit sorry for Spence when he got down on his knees with a wood chisel to chip the puppy poop off the floor. I got a bread knife out of the drawer and knelt down beside him.

He grinned at me. "You know, this is really commitment. If we can do this together, maybe we should get married." (So much for my dream of a romantic marriage proposal!)

I was stunned, and did not say yes right away, but the more I thought about it, the more I realized I'd be crazy to say no. We set the date for August 2nd, ten months away.

We both wanted our parents to be there, and since they were church-going people, we decided we needed to find a minister of some kind to do the ceremony. The only one available in August was Pastor Jack Sailor, a missionary with SEND International mission.

I was more than a bit cynical when he insisted we do six weeks of pre-marital counselling. I scoffed inwardly at most of what he and his wife said and threw the books they gave us in the garbage after only a cursory glance. But I did begin to have a begrudging respect for this couple who seemed to be committed to trying to help anyone who was in need.

The Big Old Hairy Ogre was still nattering at me, but I told myself that once I was married happiness would be within reach. I thought that would put the final magical touch on my life. Surely then this strange sense of emptiness and the feelings of inadequacy that had grown almost to the point of self-loathing would be gone. But that was not what happened.

It was about this time that my life—and my husband's life—was turned upside down. About a month before our wedding, I headed to the post office for my regular shift. Spence came with me to say hi to my boss before heading to his job on a construction site.

My boss was surprised to see us. "I didn't think you'd be in to work today," he said. "Neither of you."

I cocked my head. "Why not?"

He took a deep breath and looked at Spence. "Then you haven't heard."

It was Spence's turn to frown. "Heard what?"

"About Chuck."

"What about him?"

Another deep breath. "Chuck shot himself last night."

Spence's breath came out in whoosh. "What?"

My boss told us Chuck's wife was at his house. "Why don't you both go see how she's doing?"

We staggered out, trying to comprehend the news. Chuck was my husband's best friend. They had met when they joined the Air Force several years before, had been stationed on the same bases, made the decision to leave the armed forces together, worked in the high Arctic together and travelled to the Yukon together. They were closer than many brothers.

The next few days were intense. Robin, Chuck's wife, came to stay with us for a while, and we all tried to deal with the grief and the guilt. We were not very successful.

Why hadn't we seen it coming? Why hadn't we done something to prevent it?

Then, on the day we were married, a neighbour's baby went missing. They never found his body, but it was presumed he drowned in the Klondike River. A few months after our wedding, another friend shot himself— we later learned he had a suicide pact with Chuck—and two others died in accidents. Death became a very real presence in our lives, and we did not handle it well.

I wrote this poem to try and ease the pain:

Swamp Spruce

Two
young men
their pride in
standing
v   v
e   e
r   r
t   t
i   i
c   c
a   a
l   l

Two
black strokes
No limbs extended
to water-coloured
muskeg, meadow or sky.

Knowing, having known,
I sit staring after
the second
suicide
and I wondered
was there no answer
but
to watch them die.

When winter descended once again, we decided to try and escape the craziness of Dawson, and went off to California for a belated honeymoon. We had no idea that California would be even crazier.

It seemed everywhere we went death had gone before us. We visited a friend in Sacramento whose neighbour had been killed in a drug-related drive-by shooting. We went to Point Reyes Park north of San Francisco, where we were warned that the bodies of six women had recently been found. They had not yet caught the killer. We visited another friend and watched TV as the news crew revealed a ritual satanic murder that had just happened only one block away.

As God kept us in turmoil, Spence began asking questions. *What's life all about? What happens when we die? Where is Chuck? Where is that little baby boy? Is there a God?* Those questions plagued him until we had another significant divine appointment in our last week in California, with a retired psychiatrist who saw that Spence was deeply disturbed.

We talked into the wee hours one night, and at the end of our conversation he gave us both a book and said, "Books will be a big part of your spiritual journey." I almost scoffed out loud. Spence was not much of a reader at that time, and I did not believe we were on any kind of "spiritual journey." The BOHO and I were in agreement on that point.

But, when we returned to the Yukon, Spence began reading the book, which was about the Sermon on the Mount, the wonderful, countercultural speech in Matthew 5, in which Jesus lays out all the attributes of one who would follow Him. I watched Spence frown over it as he sat in his big chair each evening, mumbling to himself with comments like, "I didn't know the Bible said that" or "Hmmm ... interesting" and "Wow, revolutionary."

He was so intrigued by what he was reading that

he decided to meet with Jack, the missionary pastor who had performed our wedding ceremony, to discuss it. Pastor Jack met with him regularly during his lunch break for several weeks. Then Spence came home one day and told me he wanted to go to church.

I was stunned. I saw this as a potential crisis in my life. I knew my husband well enough to know that when he set his mind on a course of action, he went all the way. I feared our marriage was in danger. I thought I knew all about the "religion game" and I didn't want any part of it. Deep down I still believed I wasn't good enough for God, so I persisted in believing that He did not exist. That was preferable to believing He had rejected me. The ogre cheered me on.

But I decided to humour my husband, hoping this strange interest would eventually fade away. We began attending the Sunday morning services at the Dawson City Gospel Hall, a dilapidated old building that made me think of a haunted house.

Those Sunday mornings were very uncomfortable for me. All the members of the congregation were older than us. They dressed differently and sang songs I'd never heard before. I tried hard not to listen to anything Pastor Jack was saying. I managed to do it by making up stories in my head, which I would sometimes scribble down while Pastor Jack was speaking. I noticed others writing in small notebooks, so I knew what I was doing would easily go undetected.

After attending for a couple of months, Spence got up one Sunday morning and suggested we get ready for church. I said no and told him I had had enough of the religion game and was going to visit my friend Brenda who lived about 250 kilometers away. She had asked me to come and help her set up her weaving loom and I used that as the perfect excuse to not go to church.

"I'm done with it," I told Spence. "I don't want to go and sit with a group of people I have nothing in common with, listening to a man prattle on about things I don't believe."

At that point Spence challenged me to try and articulate what I did believe. "Is God some kind of force out there in the universe? Or is He a person you can have a relationship with, like Pastor Jack believes? What's God really like? Haven't you ever wondered? And if he exists, what does he have to do with us?"

I did not want to ponder any of those questions. The BOHO was screaming at me. "You really think any god would pay attention to someone like you?"

As I packed to go that morning, I came across the small book the psychiatrist in California had given me. It fell on the floor and opened to the words, "Why do you resist me, who flows through all things?" I tossed the book into the garbage and headed down the road to Mayo to visit my friend. I was determined not to think about spiritual things, but the harder I tried, the more all those questions kept spinning around in my head.

In frustration, I pulled into a lookout spot above the Stewart River and started talking to God. I knew I needed forgiveness. I'd heard enough of the sermons in that tiny mission church and in the classrooms of the schools I had gone to as a child, to know I had done things in my life that were against God's law, against the people around me, and even against myself. So, in a very flippant manner I told God, "Okay, go ahead and forgive me. If that's your thing, go ahead, do it!" I admitted I was confused and challenged Him to do something to prove He existed.

Then I realized that this was really crazy. Here I was, talking to a God I didn't really believe existed. I thought, *If he is out there, he must think we humans are pretty humorous.* Then something happened that is still very much a mystery to me. I *heard*, though the words were not audible, "Yes, but I love you anyway."

At that point I thought I was going crazy. Now I was hearing voices! I turned the radio on as loud as it would go so I didn't have to think and put my foot down hard on the accelerator of my truck and literally almost flew to my friend's house.

I remember pulling into the driveway and thinking, with relief, that I could leave all that religion stuff behind and just have fun weaving with Brenda. I went into the house and Brenda's husband Bruce said, "So, I hear you and Spence are going to church—what's that all about?" There's something referred to as the "moccasin telegraph" in the Yukon, which means that eventually everyone knows everyone else's business.

All we talked about that weekend was spiritual things, most of which related to eastern religions like Buddhism. By the time I headed home I had decided I definitely wanted nothing to do with Christianity and I'd just have to hope that Spence's involvement in Jack's church wouldn't tear our marriage apart. I had not been feeling well for the past while and when Brenda asked it I could be pregnant I admitted that I had wondered, but dismissed the idea

A short time later, I woke up one morning and was very ill. Then I sat down and ate a big breakfast. That was not normal for me—my breakfast was usually a cup of coffee downed on my way to work. The next day was the same, and the day after that. I finally confided in my boss at the post office that I had this strange flu. He had kind of a funny reputation in town at the time—it seemed every female he hired got pregnant soon after. (They had a great maternity plan at the post office!) So when I told him what was happening, he rolled his eyes and said, "Oh no, not again! That's morning sickness. You're pregnant!"

But I assured him that could not be. Spence and I had been together for about five years by this time. I had not told anyone, but the first desire of my heart was to have a baby. All my friends were having children and my biological clock was sounding alarms. But it was just not happening, so we decided to apply to adopt a child and were told we should have tests done to determine why we had not been able to conceive.

We travelled to Shaunessy Hospital in Vancouver. The doctors told us it was highly unlikely that we would ever conceive a child together. They called it chemical incompatibility. The Big Old Hairy Ogre was whispering again. "See? God is punishing you. You know you deserve it." We decided to pursue the adoption idea.

But that strange flu did not go away. Then one morning, as my stomach was erupting, I realized that what everyone was telling me was indeed true. I knew, with uncharacteristic certainty, that I was pregnant. And at that moment I realized God had indeed done something. He had given me the desire of my heart—a child. Katherine Melaina (our Klondike Katie) was born on November 30, 1982. I thought my heart would burst, not just with love for my first-born, but with the knowledge that I was indeed loved by God. The BOHO was, for once, silent. BOHO 0, Little Girl 101!

Not long after, the pastor in that tiny mission church asked if there was anyone in the congregation who would like to commit his life to Christ. That made me chuckle because I knew we were the only two people in that room who were not believers. I glanced at Spence, but he didn't move, so neither did I. But I started to smile because I realized we had already done that. When Spence shook Jack's hand at the door he told him we had decided to "give Jesus a try." Pastor

Jack began to weep. We were both puzzled at that. We went out for lunch and Spence voiced what I was thinking. "What's the big deal?"

As the days and weeks went by, we began to realize what the big deal was. The change in our lives was so obvious people began to comment on it. There were two women in the church who went south for the winter, as many business owners in town did, and when they came into the post office that spring I greeted them warmly as I got their mail and asked how their winter had been. When they left they had an argument. Sally thought I could not possibly be the same miserable grouchy postal employee who had been there in the fall. Betty was convinced it was me, but somehow I had really changed.

When they came to church that Sunday and saw me there, they looked at one another and smiled. Now they knew it was me—a new me. I love the scripture that says, "Therefore, if anyone is in Christ, he is a new creation; the old has passed away; behold the new has come!" (2 Corinthians 5:17, ESV). It was a visible truth in me. I was no longer that miserable grouchy postal employee, I was now a child of God who knew she was loved and accepted by a merciful God.

That spring I wrote this short poem to try and express what had happened in my heart:

First Yukon Spring

Green.
Green so fills my eyes
I sway
with spring
a song
alive and swelling
out of winter grey and white
the colour

in fields and ditches
dances
and I wonder
was there life
before this day?

There had been no real life before that day when
God drew me to Himself.

Instead of frequenting the bars, we were eager to
get together with other believers, no matter which
church they attended. We opened our home to them
all, having Friday night fellowship gatherings to sing,
pray, and talk about the Scriptures. It was an eclectic
group, spanning a wide range of ages, culture and
social status. All were invited and many attended. My
brother Terry never missed being there, and it was on
one particular Friday night that I discovered he had a
gift I did not know existed.

The gathering was smaller than usual that night,
but from the moment the first person entered our
home it was apparent something was different. We
didn't engage in any small talk as was usual but went
immediately to prayer and praise. There were silent
times as well. Then as we were praying, my brother
began to speak. I recognized his voice, but I did not
recognize nor understand the language in which he
was speaking. I was so shocked I opened my eyes to
make sure I was hearing what I thought I was. After
confirming the words were coming from his mouth, I
closed my eyes again and tried to focus on praying.

As Terry spoke my mind filled with an image that
took my breath away. It was a deep dark cave at first, then
a beam of light began to descend into it, striking several
beautiful gems below. The colours were vibrant—ruby
red, emerald green, purple amethyst, blue sapphire—
each one glowing brighter as the light spread around it.
Then another voice began to speak and again I opened

my eyes to make sure I was truly hearing our neighbour, a truck driver who I knew had little education. The words he spoke were uncharacteristically eloquent as he addressed us all, telling us we were like bright gems whose light would shine out into the world.

I had never even heard of "speaking in tongues" until that night, let alone the controversy surrounding it. I have never experienced anything like that night since. When I look back on it, I realize now that most of the people who attended that gathering were soon to leave Dawson, several of them, besides ourselves, eventually entering into full-time ministry.

Chapter 5

It was in Dawson that God began to show me that He had a plan, not only for my life but also for my writing and speaking.

I was a brand-new Christian sitting in the living room of my pastor's wife, Ella Sailor, on a cold winter's day in Dawson. We were just getting to know each other so I was more than a little intimidated by this missionary woman whose wisdom and grace were so evident.

She had just asked me if I had any hobbies. I'd had many—working with stained glass, pottery, weaving and spinning, among others. When we had a garage sale at one point, someone asked me, "Is there anything you haven't done?" But in recent days I'd realized that writing had always been of primary importance to me. I could not envision my life without it, but I rarely talked about it.

I shyly admitted, more than a little reluctantly, that I was working on writing a fantasy novel. Then I held my breath, waiting to see what Ella would say about that.

"Ah," she said, and smiled. Then she paused in a way that I was to become quite familiar with, over time. It was a pensive pause, one that meant she was considering whether or not to speak. Then she said, "I had a vision a while ago."

"A vision?" I leaned in. I'd heard about visions and, after my experience at the Friday night fellowship time, found them intriguing. Was this a normative experience for a Christian?

She nodded. "I was standing before Jesus with a stack of paper in my hands—pages of all my precious writing. Suddenly a whirlwind surrounded me and the pages began flying around. I tried to grab them, tried to hold onto them, but it was no use. The wind snatched them all away. Every single page disappeared, lost forever."

She paused again. "That's when I realized all that writing was worthless."

I almost gasped out loud.

She nodded as though she'd read my mind. "God was showing me that everything I'd written was worthless, unless it had purpose in Christ."

I leaned back and was silent. Was she telling me to stop writing all together, or just stop writing fantasy? Was she telling me writing Bible studies or missionary stories was the only thing worthy of my time?

I left her home that day pondering what her words meant for my life and, in particular, for my writing. Would I have to give up the writing I loved, now that I was a believer in Christ? It was to take me some time to sort that out. But one thing never left my mind: "be steadfast, immovable, knowing that in the Lord, your labour is not in vain" (1 Corinthians 15:58b, ESV). I had just been shown how to do a word search in the Bible, so I began to hunt for that one phrase, "in the Lord," or "in Christ," and contemplated what it really meant.

In the end, I came to the same conclusion Ella had, as the missionary-hymnwriter C.T. Studd wrote, "Only one life, 'twill soon be past, only what's done for Christ will last."

The BOHO was jeering at me, trying to convince me that I should just give up this ridiculous endeavour.

56

But I did not stop writing. Neither did I stop writing fantasy, but I was not completely sure if that was a good thing. It took some time, but eventually the moment came when I knew what God wanted me to do.

I realized, with great relief, it did not matter what form my writing took, as long as His glory was the primary goal. I realized that writing with that singular purpose in mind was the only way to ensure that my writing would never be worthless. I also began to believe, in spite of what the Big Old Hairy Ogre told me, that it also proved I was not worthless.

All that remained was for me to pray that God would show me how to accomplish His purposes through my work.

I had a friend at the time who made it her mission in life to convince me that my writing should be published, even though she'd never read anything I wrote. I had told her what my work in progress was about and that it was for children. She told me that her father knew a Christian writer who had published quite a few books for kids. She suggested I send him the manuscript I was working on. At first I refused, but she kept after me and eventually I agreed.

I did not realize who the writer was, having not grown up with Christian books as a child. One Sunday morning I mentioned his name to my pastor's wife who immediately took me into the church library and pointed out an entire shelf full of books written by that man, whose name was Bernard Palmer. She seemed quite impressed that Bernard Palmer was interested in my manuscript.

I received a few letters from Mr. Palmer and his wife, Marj, who I learned edited all his books. They were very encouraging. One of Marj's comments was especially thrilling. She said she got so caught up in the story she forgot she was supposed to be editing it. She said I should pursue publishing the book.

Unfortunately, they did not offer any ideas as to how to go about that, and I was too shy to ask, so I put their letters in a large envelope with the manuscript and it languished in a drawer for many years. The idea of publishing a book came to mind now and then, but of course the BOHO scoffed at the idea. It became something I put on the back burner, but the idea never went away.

It was about this time that the Lord began to push me in a new direction, one I would never have anticipated. It began one Sunday morning when my pastor's wife drew me aside and explained that the women of the church were planning to attend a women's retreat to be held soon, just over the border in Tok, Alaska.

"What's a women's retreat?" I asked.

Ella smiled and told me it was a time to gather with other Christian women, hear speakers, pray together, and laugh a lot.

Sounded like fun. But then Ella went on. "I wondered if you'd be willing to share your testimony at the retreat? It's usually scheduled on the first night."

"My testimony?"

She smiled again. "All you have to do is tell your story, talk about how Jesus has made a difference in your life." Ella touched my arm. "Pray about it, will you?"

I gulped and nodded.

The more I prayed the more it seemed this was something God wanted me to do. I almost told Ella "yes," but then I started second-guessing the decision. Am I just doing this to put myself out in front of these other women as someone special? The BOHO condemned and ridiculed as usual, and I almost decided I would tell Ella no. As I got ready to head to church the next Sunday, I prayed again and asked God to give me a small sign—if He wanted me to do this testimony thing, could he have Ella ask me again? If she did, I'd say "yes."

I was barely in the door when Ella approached. She asked again and I said I would do it. After all, I reasoned, it will just be a handful of women. The church in Tok couldn't be much bigger than ours.

So it was, I found myself climbing into a small Cessna airplane, wondering what on earth I would say when it came time for me to tell my story. I kept calming myself down by telling myself it would just be a small gathering. Writing things down also helped to calm my nerves.

We were picked up at the airport and taken to the Tok high school where the meeting was to be held. I'm sure my jaw dropped open when I stepped through the door. The gymnasium was packed with women from all over Alaska and the Yukon. My knees began to shake, and I wondered if it was too late to back out. Only the thought of disappointing Ella kept me from doing so. I wandered among the women, feeling more than a little like a fish out of water.

Then I saw her. She was tall for an indigenous woman, with a calm face, intense eyes, and a long thick braid hanging down her back. We made eye contact and, for some reason, I was reassured. This was where God wanted me to be. I was not able to get close enough to speak to that lady, but we seemed to constantly be connected as the evening wore on.

Then it was testimony time.

I stood before all those women with my hands in my pockets and my eyes on the floor. When I finished there wasn't a sound from the large gathering. I shuffled back to my seat and was amazed when several women crowded around me, saying thank you and other words of encouragement. I felt someone's hands on my shoulders and heard a soft mumbling. I turned my head enough to see it was that tall indigenous woman. She moved away before I could speak to her.

The rest of the weekend blessed me in many ways. It was thrilling to realize that "the church" was much bigger than our small congregation in Dawson. The stories I heard inspired me and the prayer times strengthened me. It seemed to end too soon.

When we arrived at the airport I saw that lovely woman sitting alone and approached her tentatively. She smiled and nodded when I sat down beside her. I asked where she lived and she told me the name of the small village on the Yukon River. "I love the river," I said.

Her smile widened. "Oh, yes, every morning I wake up and look out at the river and thank our Jesus." She turned toward me. "You will have a speaking ministry. God will bless others through your words." Then she stood and walked away to board her plane.

I pondered her words as we flew back to Dawson, wondering what she meant by "a speaking ministry." The following Sunday pastor Jack chatted with a few women in the foyer. When I joined them, he smiled at me and said, "And I hear we have a speaker in our midst." I literally looked over my shoulder, thinking he was talking about someone else. Oh me, of little faith.

About two years after we became believers, my husband began to feel the need to study more of the Bible. Pastor Jack agreed and started praying. We hadn't told anyone else what we were thinking, but one Sunday morning when the pastor asked if anyone had anything they wanted to share, a woman stood up and said, "Yes, Spence has something to tell us."

Spence gaped. "I do?" But he stood up and stammered, "Uh, yeah, well, Marcie and I are thinking about going to Bible College." As the congregation applauded, Spence plopped down into the seat again. He told me later his first thought was, "Oh wow, now we have to do it!"

Not long after that our mailbox was jammed with brochures from Bible colleges all over North America. I thought someone had used one of the cards that were often inserted in Christian magazines to sign us up for "more information." But no one in the church would admit to doing it.

Spence poured over the brochures. Alaska Bible College, just a short flight away, seemed like a good fit, so Spence decided to go and check it out. Clayton, a friend from church, went along to give moral support. Spence came home and told me he didn't think that was where God wanted us. Clayton came home and told his wife to start packing because "we're going to Bible College!"

Pastor Jack recommended his alma mater, Briercrest, the largest Bible college in Canada. Spence kept shaking his head. "Too far away and too big," he said, until the day his sister called to find out what he was up to and I heard him say, "Yeah, it looks like we're going to move to Saskatchewan." My eyebrows shot up when he hung up the phone. He grinned a little sheepishly. "Well, at least it's in Canada."

When he confessed his fear and trembling to Pastor Jack and explained that he'd never been very good at academics, the wise pastor suggested he take a couple of courses by correspondence to test the waters. Spence not only thoroughly enjoyed those courses, he aced them and began to think maybe he could do this after all.

But how? Bible college was expensive and we had never been very good at saving money. We prayed some more and realized the only way to do it was to sell our home. We did not think that would be a problem. Many people had told us, "If you ever want to sell, please let me know." We let them all know but no one came knocking.

The summer was just getting under way when a young couple came by and made us a good offer. They moved onto the property, made our shed livable for the summer, planted the garden and the greenhouse and paid us rent in fish. I started canning salmon. It was the end of July when they came to us again and admitted their financing had fallen through. We tried hard to spread the word that the house was for sale again, but, again, no one came knocking.

We were beginning to feel the clock ticking when a First Nations couple who attended our church mentioned they might be interested. We invited them out to chat. They came and we had a great evening talking about the Lord, but they didn't ask any questions about the house. We assumed they were not interested.

About the middle of August, a man came to see us who had just been hired as the butcher in town. He wanted to rent the house. We hadn't thought of doing that but decided it would work. He wanted us to draw up a lease, but we said, oh no, we didn't need to do that. That wasn't the Yukon way. We shook hands and assumed it was all settled.

I started packing in earnest. We mailed all of our belongings to Saskatchewan. Then, on August 17th, which is the day Dawson celebrates the discovery of gold, Spence took the last of our boxes, containing our kitchen, to the post office and went over to the grocery store to drop off the key to the butcher. He shook his head sheepishly and said he and his wife were out for a walk the night before and saw a place for rent in town and decided that would suit them better. They had rented it that morning. "Sorry," he said.

Spence was stunned. Katie, our two-year-old at the time, was waiting in the car. He got into the driver's seat and sat there for a while, wondering what on earth he should do. Should he go and ask the post office to give us our kitchen back? He started to pray and literally took his hands off the steering wheel and asked God to show him what to do.

A friend tapped on the window and told Spence the parade had just ended and he should take Katie over to see the floats and join in the kids' games. That was the last thing Spence felt like doing, but he put the car in gear and drove to the park. There was a parking space right in front of it—a miracle in itself, because of the number of people in town celebrating.

He got out of the vehicle and Eldria Christiansen, who had come to talk to us about the house way back in the spring, was standing right there. She smiled and said, "Oh, I'm glad I bumped into you. Art had a dream last night that we should buy your house! He's over there helping with the kids' games." More stunned than ever, Spence walked over and talked to him. He said he'd come out to the house at 6:00 that night to talk to us about it.

Spence came home and told me he had good news and bad news. When he told me what had happened, I shrugged and said, "Well, I don't know what the Lord's doing, but I'm packing." There was a going away barbecue for us that night. We decided Spence would stay at the house and wait for Art while I went to the party. Six o'clock came. No sign of Art. 6:30, 7:00. Spence thought Art had changed his mind, so he got down on his knees and prayed in the middle of our empty living room. He told God he was giving up, that he would do whatever He wanted us to do. If that was to stay in Dawson and look like fools that was okay, we'd do it. If it was to go to Briercrest without selling the house, we'd do that. Spence said he literally threw up his hands and said, "You are our God, no matter what. Just tell me what you want us to do."

Then he heard the loose board thump on the bridge into our property and he heard a truck. Art arrived with a cheque in his hand for a down payment. They shook hands and agreed on a payment schedule for the rest. Spence arrived at the barbecue and told me it was okay—we could carry on with the going away party. We were indeed going away.

A few days later we left for Bible College with two little girls, a husky dog, and the rest of our earthly belongings packed into an old station wagon. The sale of the house gave us just enough money to live for three years. Spence did the four-year program in three, and I managed to cram in a few classes in between his. He would literally run home when his class ended to take care of our two little girls while I ran to my class.

Sometimes this resulted in hilarious though embarrassing incidents. One mid-winter day Spence burst through the front door to find me still in my jeans and a T-shirt. "Aren't you going to your class?"

I gasped. I'd been writing and had forgotten all about the class in Romans with Dr. Henry Hildebrand, the school's chancellor. I leaped up, pulled my skirt out of the dryer, threw it on, and raced out the door. There was only one seat left in the room, in the middle of the front row.

It wasn't until I was seated that I realized something was amiss. I seemed to be sitting on something lumpy. I wiggled around as discreetly as I could until the lump fell on the floor. I scooped up the sock and stuffed it in my purse. But there were other lumps—four in all, that needed to be dealt with. By this time the young men sitting around me were snickering and Dr. Hildebrandt was frowning. I was glad when the class ended and I headed for the door. That's when I felt a whoosh as something else fell from inside my skirt—my husband's underwear! I know my face was bright red as I scooped it up and fled.

We were at the end of those three years at Briercrest when a friend asked me to attend a seminar being put on by Carol Kent called Speak Up with Confidence. I declined, mostly because of our lack of finances, which had been almost totally depleted by the end of those three years. When my friend offered to pay for the course, I gave in. I told my friend that I had no intension of ever becoming a public speaker. The experience at the Tok Retreat had faded to a dream-like memory. (Oh me, of little faith!) But my friend still insisted.

As Carol Kent talked, giving tips on public speaking, she talked a lot about the process of writing. It was during one of those sessions that the proverbial lightbulb went off in my brain and I realized that I could and should use this passion I had for writing to help build the kingdom of God on earth.

As I grew as a Christian, I began to write as a believer in Jesus, realizing that He is the author of my life—the One who knows my story from beginning to end, because He wrote it himself. It's astonishing to think that God had my life planned before I was born. The prophet Jeremiah said God told him that "Before I formed you in the womb I knew you" (Jeremiah 1:5, ESV). I don't think Jeremiah was special. I think God knows each and every one of us in that same deeply intimate way. He knew me in my mother's womb, when the perverted man touched me, when I was watching those high school teachers, when I walked away from God, and when I cried out to him on the road to Mayo. And God had a plan.

He knew me when I read *Emily of New Moon*, and when Mrs. Burgess made that statement that stopped me from writing. He knew me when I chose Journalism over Honours English and when I sat by that wood stove and wrote my first novel. He knew me when that fire was ignited inside me at the Speak Up with Confidence seminar. But again, I had no idea what to do about it. I didn't have any idea how to begin, but God was about to show me the way.

Chapter 6

If there is one thing I've learned as a writer struggling to get my books out to people who need them, it's that God does have a plan and leads us into it so that, as Psalm 26:7 says, we may go about "proclaiming aloud your praise and telling of all your wonderful deeds" (NIV).

When my husband and I went to Bible college we purchased an old Brother typewriter. We thought it was awesome because it had a small screen that showed you what you had just typed so you could make changes before going on.

But it took a special kind of paper and over time the type faded, the words disappeared. I discovered this one day when I opened a folder of essays I had written and chosen to keep. The paper had turned a shiny grey and the type was almost completely invisible. And I was upset. There were no other copies of those essays. It made me realize that one day all of my words would be gone. The ogre's mocking voice screamed, "Your words don't matter. No one will ever care about them. See? They're just going to fade away."

But now there was another voice that made me realize that my words were a legacy and a testimony to God's grace and mercy that would live on through the lives of those who had been touched and changed by them.

As my husband was about to graduate from Briercrest Bible College, we began praying about what might be next. Did God want us on the mission field? I found that prospect enticing and so did Spence, but as we prayed and talked to the profs and others who had gotten to know us, we were advised to get a grounding in a local church first. That meant exploring the idea of going into pastoral ministry.

We quickly discovered there were more denominations than bees in a swarm and trying to sort them out made our heads spin. Spence was invited to preach at a few churches in the area, but none of them seemed to be a good fit. We continued to pray but felt no clear direction.

But God had a plan and another divine appointment in mind. It took the form of a pastor and leader in the Associated Gospel Churches of Canada. His name was Bud Penner. After a few conversations with Bud we made arrangements to candidate at a small church in Ponoka, Alberta. That meant engaging in a trial run, of sorts. Spence would preach and lead in communion.

Arrangements were made for us to meet with as many of the elders and members of the church as possible over a weekend. We met with one of the founding members, a woman who told us her name was Mrs. Johnston. "And you may call me Mrs. Johnston."

We had dinner on a five-generational farm where I visited with the grandma, who was churning butter in the kitchen, while the men invited Spence to help dig a silage pit. We had lunch at another farm where the eldest son named all the cattle as we rode among them. By the end of that weekend we felt as though we had known these people for years. We even remembered their names, something that had never come easily to either of us. We returned to Briercrest and waited for the call.

I started to fret a bit. Well, okay, more than a bit, mostly due to that wretched BOHO who kept telling me we would not be good enough for that church. Our finances were drained to the point where it looked like we'd be eating macaroni at every meal for the next while. And how would we move when/if the time came? We couldn't afford a mover, let alone a damage deposit and rent for a house. And what about furniture? All we had was a small kitchen table and two worn-out living room chairs. We'd need beds and a dining room table so we could have our new congregants over for meals. How would we manage all that? The BOHO told me it was impossible.

Then I remembered how God had provided for us over the past three years. I asked forgiveness, and the ability to trust Him with our future. And I tried not to listen to the BOHO.

My hand shook a bit when I retrieved a card in our box at the post office soon after. It was for a registered letter. *This could be it*, I thought. But the postmistress handed me a brown envelope from the Yukon Territorial Government. It informed Spence that a union he had belonged to when he worked at the nursing station in Dawson had finally signed their agreement. I was a bit disgusted that they wasted the cost of a registered letter to inform us about something that no longer concerned us.

About a week later we received another card for a registered letter. I was more than a little disgruntled this time, to discover it too was from the Territorial Government, and almost tossed it in the garbage when I got home. But since it was addressed to my husband, I put it on the counter and almost forgot to mention it when he came in for lunch. He opened it to find a cheque for $250. We were thrilled. No more macaroni. A few days later another cheque arrived, then another for over $1,000. Spence was so sure it was a mistake he called the government offices in Whitehorse and asked them to check. A pleasant voice informed him that no, there was no mistake, and there would be more money coming our way. Over time we received more than enough to get completely set up in a new home.

Then we received a phone call from the chairman of the board at the church where we had candidated, inviting Spence to become their senior pastor. A few weeks later four men arrived with a horse trailer, loaded up all our personal belongings and led the way to the heart of Alberta's cowboy country.

The previous pastor, who was planning to remain in the church, met with Spence and gave him the list of all the things he was now responsible for. The list was long—that pastor had been a "one man show." He did everything, including make the bulletin on an ancient Gestetner. Just as they were about to say good-bye, the pastor said, "Oh, and by the way, you have to write a weekly column in the newspaper and it's due tomorrow."

Spence came home with his mind in a whirl and asked if I could write the column. That was the beginning of *The Spur*, taken from Hebrews 10:24: "Let us consider how we may spur one another on toward love and good deeds." Since we were now living in a stampede town (second only to the Calgary Stampede), I thought it would be an appropriate title.

That column ran in two local newspapers for about eighteen years and was also picked up by a coffee news publication (one of those one page things that you often see in coffee shops), that was distributed throughout Alberta and Saskatchewan. The Lord graciously opened the door and showed me how to step through it.

Soon after settling into Ponoka, I discovered there was a Christian writers organization called Alberta Christian Writers' Fellowship. I went to a small seminar they held just north of where we lived and was totally thrilled to meet others of like mind and belief. God opened another door, one which put me on the path of learning once again, as I attended conferences and workshops that continued to teach me the skills I needed to write well.

Within that first year I was asked to join the executive, holding several different positions over the years, including president for several terms. During that time the group expanded to a Canada-wide organization and changed its name to InScribe Christian Writers' Fellowship. I attribute a good deal of my growth both as a writer and as a believer to that group.

In a way, I also believe InScribe kept me sane. The people in the church where we pastored at the time did not relate well to having a pastor's wife who sat at home writing. Most of them felt I was wasting my time and should have been out doing other, more "redeeming" things. Any time I mentioned my writing I was met with blank stares at best, or outright disapproval on occasion. The BOHO was now not just a figment of my imagination, but at times a real live disapproving human being. Attending WorDshops and conferences where I met people who understood and affirmed my choice to write, was not only a great relief, it was a life-saving experience. When I became frustrated or was hurt by something said or done, there were people within InScribe who were there to keep me from despair.

It was at InScribe events that I was introduced to resources that led to publication. I learned about *The Christian Writer's Market Guide*, for instance. I studied that book and began writing Sunday School papers for Cook Publications and others and had stories and articles published in magazines. I also did some journalistic writing for local and provincial newspapers. A few of my pieces, including poetry, were broadcast on CBC radio.

God also had more divine appointments scheduled for me. It was at an InScribe conference that I first met a man named Gus Henne who was working with a small publishing company in Ontario. After a long conversation with Gus, he convinced me to publish my first devotional book, *Spur of the Moment*—a compilation of the articles written for those local newspapers. I was terrified of embarking on such a risky venture. I'd heard many stories about people who had published a book only to have it remain in boxes in their basement or garage.

But, for some time, people had been asking me to put the column into book form so they could give it to family and friends. So, after a lot of prayer, Gus's prodding, and my husband's support, *Spur of the Moment* was released in 2002. In spite of a terrible cover, the book won an Award of Merit at Write Canada and sold well. I began to receive emails and phone calls from all over the province and beyond, telling me how my words had been a blessing. A second edition, with a new cover designed by my daughter Laura, was published a few years later. That book is now in its third edition and, Lord willing, may soon be republished under a different title and cover.

I recently received an email from a woman who works for two elderly ladies in their 90s. She said she was walking by their room one day and heard them giggling. It was not a common occurrence, so she stepped in to see what they were laughing about. They were reading one of the stories in *Spur of the Moment* and told her how much they were being blessed by the book. Another woman emailed to tell me that she had purchased the devotional when it was first published and had read it several times over the last few years. She was reading it again and wrote to tell me how much it was still blessing her. It is such an encouragement to me that even after a span of more than twenty years,

God is still using that book to be a blessing to those who read it. For a while the Big Old Hairy Ogre almost disappeared.

Another divine appointment came when I enrolled in a class at Red Deer College, taught by local writer Sigmund Brouwer. Sigmund asked each of us to show him something we had recently written, so he could get an idea of what level we were at, as he put together the lessons he would teach. I handed in a short story. The next week he approached me and asked if that story had been published. I was stunned and said no. He told me he thought it was ready to go and I should look for a publisher. I doubt Sigmund knew how much of an encouragement that was to me. I sent the story off and was thrilled when it was accepted for publication. Sigmund has been a friend, encourager, and mentor to me ever since, though probably unwittingly so.

All of these incidents, and the people who were in them, helped me to listen more closely to that "other voice"—one that silenced the ogre, one that built me up with encouragement and prodded me to keep putting my words out there, because He had purpose in them. I began to believe that His purposes included a role I was to play as a scribe for His kingdom, recording the wonders of His creation and the holiness of His being.

Chapter 7

My little girl stood alone on the stage, her body rigid, her eyes round and frightened as she waited for the signal to begin. When it came, she took a deep breath and sang. Her voice was quite soft, she swayed a little and wrung her hands, but she got through it, then waited again, as she'd been instructed, while the adjudicator finished making notes. She remained motionless as the judge told her what she thought. The comments were kind and I breathed a sigh of relief. When my ten-year-old came back to her seat I put my arm around her. "Good job, Laura," I said.

She shrugged my hand away, put both of her hands under her legs and shook her head. "I'm never ever, ever, ever doing that again!" Then she burst into tears.

About seven years later I watched with pride and not a little amazement as Laura sang the lead role in her high school production of *The Wizard of Oz*. She had come a long way since that day when she performed her first solo in front of an audience, before an adjudicator at that music festival. In the years since, she has sung countless times on a stage and joined a worship band in our church. The journey wasn't easy for her. She had to learn how to get over being so terribly nervous, how to stand still, how to breathe and project her voice. But she had good teachers and many who encouraged her along the way. We've laughed more than once about that day when she said "never ever again."

I have to acknowledge that I too have been there. With fear and trepidation, I've sent my work out to a publisher only to get a scathing critique back. The BOHO was quick to attack, and I tucked that manuscript away and said "never ever, ever, again." It has only been through prayer, and the help of other writers that I have conquered those disappointments, worked through the fear and did do it again, and again, and again. Perseverance is key in writing as in life and in spiritual development. As someone once said, the only failure is the one who quits.

I take cues on this from many characters in the Bible, characters who failed badly but did not let those failures keep them from moving forward into the plans and purposes God had for their lives. Characters like Moses, Abraham, David, Peter, and Paul. They were destined to do great things for God, in spite of their weaknesses and failures. I expect they all had their own BOHOs. No doubt they all wanted to say "never again" at some point, but they all knew there was One they could turn to, One who would forgive and empower and strengthen. They admitted their weaknesses, took counsel from those who guided them back to God, and then they kept going.

Though he was facing death, the apostle Paul said, "I consider my life worth nothing to me; my only aim is to finish the race and complete the task the Lord Jesus has given me—the task of testifying to the gospel of God's grace" (Acts 20:24, NIV).

As a writer who is Christian, I too have been given that task of testimony, whether I do it through articles in magazines, poems posted on blogs, or novels sent out to publishers. I too am to testify to the grace and mercy and glory of God. Until He comes again or transports me to stand before Him, I must persevere.

He taught me this important lesson one day when I was a struggling art student. I was not very good at drawing. In fact, when I realized I had to take the drawing class as part of the art program I had signed up for, and that it was held at eight o'clock in the morning, I was blunt with my instructor.

"I don't do mornings," I told him, "so don't expect me to be wide awake and ready to draw at 8:00 in the morning. And by the way, I can't even draw a stick figure to save my life."

He smiled and assured me he would have me drawing well and loving it, by the end of that first term. I was skeptical but he was right. I remember one particular session that not only taught me how to draw, it helped me to learn how to draw closer to God and to my dad.

The instructor often brought in live models for us to sketch but on this particular day, he pushed a desk to the middle of the room and sat on it. "I'm your model today," he said, and explained a technique called line drawing. The idea was to look only at the figure being drawn, never at the paper. Without lifting the pencil, we were to draw the subject with a single continuous line. My first attempts were pitiful, but the instructor encouraged us to keep trying. Sheets of paper fell to the floor all over the studio as the students attempted to copy what was before them.

As I worked, I began to realize how staring at an object for that long, with that much concentration, helps you see things you would not have otherwise noticed. Trying to make that continuous line look like the man on the desk was a challenge, but the more I tried, the more I realized it wasn't impossible.

Later that evening, while watching TV with my father, he fell asleep in his chair. I quietly pulled out paper and a graphite stick and did a line drawing of him. It was, in a way, a moment of enlightenment. The more I tried to copy him, the more I saw things I had never noticed before—how long his fingers were, how crooked the leg broken when he was a teenager. As I concentrated on him, I began to see the real man, not just a superficial impression of him. I began to realize too, the benefit of not looking at what my hand was drawing. The point was not to achieve perfection, but to capture the essence of the subject.

I needed that perspective. As every child does, I longed for my father's attention and approval. I rarely received it. He was not a cruel man, by any means, but he did not involve himself in the lives of his children. It was the era when the husband "brought home the bacon," and the wife raised the kids. I took his aloofness to mean rejection and for many years I harboured a deep resentment toward him because of it.

That exercise of drawing my dad opened my eyes to his humanity, to his frailty. I began to see him, not as a man who had failed to give me the emotional support I needed, but a man who was himself broken. I was to learn more about that brokenness some time later, when I wrote a play about his experience during World War 2. (More about that later.) Though I did not realize it then, that night was a step toward forgiveness and a resolve to keep trying to bond with him. This is how I expressed it:

Line Drawing

Graphite feeds
a soft black line onto white paper.
I must never look away
but move my hand around his form
continuously, smooth reality
into art
starting with the chair, his chair,
high backed, footrest up,
my line edges his leg, bends over his knee,

the unnatural angle
of one leg broken long ago.

I loosen my grip,
loop the folds of his sweater, baggy
over his arm, descend to the
hand, short-lined fingers curled,
pipe cradled in the palm.

One quick stroke cuts
across his stomach, belting him in
then softens again to fold the other arm
and on to his shoulder, slouched,
the chin on chest,
glasses tipped forward.

I round his nose
sweep back his hair in
one final black wave and
the flow of line is over.

But I dare not look away, aware
I have begun to see
I have created
my father.

That day often comes to mind and makes me realize
that perseverance is an essential part of the writing life.
If I had allowed frustration at my lack of drawing skill to
stop me, I would never have known what I was capable
of and I would never have known the joy that comes
through the process. Perseverance, in learning to draw
and in learning to write, led to more skills learned, which
led to results I could be proud of. Perseverance in my
relationship with my father eventually led to healing.

Chapter 8

In the film, *Hurricane*, there's a thread that warms my heart as a writer. A young man whose life is full of distress, picks a book from a bin at a second-hand store and takes it home. The book not only changes his life, but, because he is moved to connect with its author, in prison for a crime he did not commit, it changes the writer's life too.

When the young man and the writer meet, Hurricane Carter asks him, "Do you think it was an accident you picked up my book?" Hurricane implies it was not. He implies it was in God's plan. The book was meant for that young man. It set him on a path, a journey designed for him.

I have often seen God work that way. He has put things and people in my path, which gave me exactly what I needed for that time in my life. Some years ago, just after God had opened the door for me to publish my faith column in our local newspaper, I was on the campus of a nearby Bible school with my husband. He was not having a good day. I don't remember what the issue was, but his mood was decidedly dark.

We went into the campus bookstore and I headed for the bin of reduced items. Right on the top was a book called *Writing Religiously* by Don M. Aycock and Leonard G. Goss. I snapped it up, thrilled that I'd found something that seemed to confirm what I believed God was telling me to do—write for the building of His kingdom.

I showed the book to my husband. His reaction was not very polite. In fact, it stunned me with its harshness. I don't remember his exact words, but it was to the effect that this was just another hobby I'd soon give up.

Please know this was not characteristic of my husband. In fact, I can't remember another time when he has ever spoken to me the way he did that day. I was so stunned and angry that I put the book back and left the store.

A few moments later he joined me, book in hand, and apologized. We then had a "clear the air" kind of conversation in which I told him how much writing meant to me now that I had become a believer. It was the first time I told him that I believed writing was my calling, in the same way that he was called to be a pastor.

I believe that day and that conversation were meant to happen. That book was waiting for me. It was the spark that launched my career, and my husband's response, though it was harsh, was the spark that gave me the determination to begin. God knew exactly what I needed at that time in my life.

A friend recently sent me this quote: "And in Bible-story journeys, ain't no journey hopeless. Everybody find what they supposed to find" (from *Sounder* by William H. Armstrong).

Talk to anyone who reads the Bible regularly and they will tell you that statement is more than true. The Bible story journeys and, indeed, the journeys we discover in other books we read, are meant for each and every one of us. They will provide the hope, the joy, and sometimes just the dogged determination we need to keep going on the path we are meant to follow.

God's timing is always perfect. As I look out at my surroundings today, the colour green has never seemed more beautiful. The tree in front of our house is about to come into full leaf. The freshness of new buds bursting delights the eyes. Perhaps it seems all the more wonderful because it was a long time coming.

We've had a cool spring this year, with big fluffy flakes of white stuff piling up on our lawn even into May. But even though the days were cool and the nights frosty, you could see the change happening in the trees and bushes all around. I found myself delighting in it each day as the willows turned red and the grey poplars darkened, moving steadily toward maturity in spite of the weather. Though the days have been grey, I knew the sap was stirring. Now that the sun has finally arrived the trees are bursting out with new growth. Their time has arrived.

It makes me think of the long process toward maturity as a writer. The road has seemed hard and the desired end result a long time coming, but like the trees around us there is growth and progress, even though the environment doesn't seem to be cooperative.

I know God's hand is moving me along the path toward becoming a mature Christian and a mature writer as surely as he is directing the course of the seasons. The blossoming of the trees and flowers is never late, in God's timing. Neither is the timing of my "arrival" as a writer.

I was encouraged recently to read about Josie Neill, a Scottish woman who published her first book of poetry at the age of 86. Then there's Madeleine L'Engle, whose book *A Wrinkle in Time* was rejected 26 times. Tolkien's books, *The Hobbit* and *The Lord of the Rings*, were ignored by the New York Times when published and did not receive notoriety until the 1960s. And then there's Herman *Mody Dick* was a total failure when it was first published, and *Billy Budd* did not become popular until after his death.

The first edition of *Chicken Soup for The Soul* was rejected 144 times.

I have come to recognize that rejections give further resolve to work harder and that God is in control. He has a plan and a timeline for my work. Friends give the encouragement that keeps me going when I'm discouraged. And those wonderful moments of accomplishment silence the BOHO and give a sense of awe and even humility as I recognize the hand of God in it all. And I keep going. I keep writing. It's for me to keep moving forward, persevering as I learn the craft, and rejoicing as He uses my gifts to His purposes. And taking joy in the journey.

But it is so very easy to slip off the path God has laid out for me to follow. I listened to a rather good sermon recently that made me sit up and take notes. We were visiting the church we planted in Blackfalds, Alberta, nineteen years ago. It was wonderful to see the church still thriving and to know we had left it in good hands with a pastor whose heart is obviously seeking God's will. At one point during the sermon he said, "Let go of the gift. Worship the Giver." It was one of those moments when I knew God was speaking directly to me. I almost gasped, sat back in my chair and pondered. *Have I been doing that?* I realized there have been times when I have focused too much on the gift, which has led to the appearance of those ugly twins, pride and arrogance.

As I thought about it I realized that too many times I have worshiped the gift instead of the Giver, gotten caught up in the thrill of writing, let arrogance creep in, and lost track of what my true purpose is, to reveal the goodness of God and the depth of His grace and mercy.

This is the calling, the privilege, to walk forward in faith, in that calling, for, as George Herbert's wonderful little poem, "The Temple," says,

Of all the creatures in the sea and land
Only to Man thou hast made known thy ways,
and put the pen alone into his hand,
and made him Secretary of thy praise.

I once read a short essay about how an author had broken free of writer's block. I don't remember her name, but I remember the way she expressed how she was energized again and proclaimed, "The goal, to write. The prize, to publish."

I felt like cheering. To write—yes! A worthy goal. To publish—yes! And it was here that I paused.

The question came to mind—what is the prize? Is it seeing your byline in a magazine or newspaper or on the cover of a book? Is it receiving a cheque for a piece of writing you have laboured over? I've had the thrill of all of these, and yes, it is a thrill, but it is fleeting. The byline may not be noticed nor remembered. The cheque evaporates like mist. Surely there is more.

Is the prize perhaps the process itself? Is the prize all that is learned along the way? Is the prize the life being lived as a writer who belongs to Christ and discovering that my words have made a difference? Yes, yes, and yes!

Henri Nouwen wrote,

Writing is a process in which we discover what lives within us. The writing, itself, reveals what is alive! The deepest satisfaction of writing is precisely that it opens up new spaces within us of which we were not aware before we started to write. To write is to embark on a journey whose final destination we do not know.

What lives within me—that which is alive—is revealed as I write. As those spaces open up within me, I discover Who will fill them. As I trust Him, not

85

knowing the destination becomes irrelevant. He knows the beginning and the end of my stories and my life.

What greater prize can there be? When I focus on the Spirit of God as the giver and sustainer of the gift, it is as I write that I understand Who that Spirit is. It is as I build my stories, my articles, my poems, that I discover the depth of His wisdom and love.

That journey, that adventure is in itself a gift. I pray that I would own no other prize.

God has often given me that joy which comes when I am on track, following His guidance. He has also, when needed, made sure my pride and arrogance are dealt with.

When I was asked to teach a workshop on writing devotions at an InScribe conference not long after joining the organization, I was thrilled. And I confess I developed a rather *bik hed* (big head) as they say in Papua New Guinea. My ego swelled to rather dangerous proportions as I watched the students arrive and take their places at the table. There was one elderly woman whom I pinpointed as she took her seat. *She's probably writing little stories for her grandkids,* I thought. *Isn't that sweet.*

I blush to think of it now, and I smile ruefully at myself when I think of how God orchestrated a way to deal with my sin. I ended up sitting beside that woman at the lunch table. I asked what she was working on, expecting the response I'd imagined earlier.

"Well, at the moment I'm editing a Greek manuscript by [insert the name of a very well renowned theologian]."

"Oh?" I'm sure my shock was evident. "And how is that going?"

She smiled indulgently. "I'm having to make quite a few corrections."

I felt like crawling under the table and I'm sure my face was quite red. The BOHO was taunting again.

86

"How arrogant you are! How can God use a person like you?"

I reminded him of all the amazing people in the Bible who were, like me, full of the pride that we all struggle with, yet God used them. That day was a lesson I've never forgotten. I've often thanked God for being so gracious to me in the way He dealt with my arrogance and pride.

But I often need reminders.

I was inching forward in the drive-thru at Tim' Horton's coffee shop one day and feeling a little sorry for myself. Well, okay, maybe a little more than a little. I'd had an email from my publisher telling me a statement of the sales for my novel, *One Smooth Stone*, was on its way. He also said the sales "weren't what we were hoping for." As I pondered what that meant I sighed, noting he had not mentioned a royalty cheque.

Good thing I had just signed on to begin a new job, stocking book racks for a small distribution company. The books were all Christian and the money was surprisingly good, but in my pity-party mood I grumbled about helping to sell other people's books instead of my own. I wondered if God was trying to humble me.

Just as that thought came into my head, I pulled alongside a large garbage bin. A woman dressed in the Tim's uniform approached it at the same time. She was attractive, even in the uniform, and looked just a bit younger than me. She tugged the large bag out of the receptacle and went about replacing it with a new one.

Well, at least I'm not doing that, I thought. Then she looked up and gave me the most amazing beaming smile. I recovered from my shock just in time to smile back.

As I drove away sipping my coffee, I pondered what had just happened. That woman's beaming smile told me that she did not consider it demeaning in any way to be changing that garbage bag. I don't know if she was a believer in Christ, but she certainly seemed to have His attitude about service.

And I was humbled. I realized God was trying to wake me up to the fact that being content and even happy doesn't depend on what my work is or on how many books I sell, it depends on what I believe about myself and about Him. I began to examine those two things in relation to one another. Who am I? A child of Christ, loved beyond measure and blessed to an abundance that is staggering. What do I believe about God? That He wants only my good and will move heaven and earth to bring me to an awareness of His goodness and glory. BOHO 0, Little Girl Writer 1001!

And then, I forgot again!

InScribe Christian Writers' Fellowship had just initiated the Janette Oke Award. When I saw the announcement, I smiled. *This one is in the bag*, I thought. I filled out the application, totally confident that I would win it. After all, who else in that organization had given more to the group? I'd been a member for over thirty years, on the executive in some capacity for a good part of that time and served as a volunteer and teacher at many of their conferences.

Shortly after I sent the application, I was asked to judge a category in the contest, as I had many times in the past. I awarded the first, second and third prizes and sent the results to the coordinator. She called me soon after and asked if I would consider switching the first and second place winners. I thought it was an odd request and asked why. She explained they wanted to spread the love as much as possible and since the first-place winner was going to be awarded the Janette Oke Award, they felt the change would be appropriate.

I was speechless. How dare they? After all I'd given to that group! I mumbled a vague yes and hung up. The anger raging inside me became obvious and my husband asked what was wrong. I spewed out all the vile things I was thinking. He listened patiently, then said, "Have you thought to ask yourself why you're so angry about this?" I gave him my list but he did not accept it. "I think there's something deeper," he said. Eventually I admitted that the root of it was that I took it personally, as though they were saying, "You're just not good enough. You need to try harder." It's another of the lies that I've been prone to believe all my life.

One of the things that chafed was the fact that the woman who had won the award was a friend and very much deserving of it. In fact, as I came to admit eventually, she was the perfect candidate. Sitting in the audience watching Janette Oke give the award to my friend was not easy but by then God had been working on my heart and I was able to smile and congratulate her sincerely. My sour grapes were slowly being turned into sweet wine and once again the BOHO was silenced. Soli Deo Gloria.

It is situations like that which make me consider my motivations, my need for man's approval. It makes me realize the need to be vigilant, to guard against my own nature, to strive to follow God's agenda rather than my own.

Some years ago I watched a video that I'd heard a lot about. People said it was inspiring. They said I just had to watch it. Sometimes I ignore these kinds of messages, but eventually I gave in and clicked into the YouTube channel to see what all the fuss was about.

The small screen showed a rather plump, unassuming middle-aged man with crooked teeth. He stood at a microphone looking decidedly unsure of himself. Then the camera panned to the four judges watching him. Their expressions seemed to say, *Let's just get this over with.* Finally one of them asked why he was there. "To sing opera," he said simply. The judges smirked. One of them rolled his eyes. But they let him go ahead.

Then the man opened his mouth, and his voice boomed out as he sang from his heart and soul. The judges' jaws dropped. Some in the audience began to weep; so did one of the judges. When he was done, the audience was on its feet cheering for the cell phone salesman who had just demonstrated that you can't always tell a book by its cover.

The man's name was Paul Potts and he went on to win the competition called *Britain's Got Talent*. He became a star and continues to sing around the world for large audiences. His is a fairytale, rags-to-riches success story that has captured the imagination of millions. It made me wonder why. Why have so many, and I count myself among them, responded so strongly to Mr. Potts' performance?

I think it's because all of us have a tiny part in us that says, "There's something great in me too, if I can just find a way to let everyone see it." Some might call that arrogance and delusions of grandeur. I think it's something more. I think it's a deep belief that we are more than we seem to be. Because we are.

When God created the first man He "breathed into his nostrils the breath of life" (Genesis 2:7, NIV). He also created him "in his own image" (Genesis 1:27). Humanity is much more than just a bunch of bones, tissue, and blood. We were created to house the very spirit of God himself, to be a temple and in a sense a representative of God. I think we all feel that and long for it to be fulfilled—it's a longing for the nobility, the beauty, even the glory we were intended to have as children of a most merciful God.

I feel it, this longing for greatness. I strive for excellence in my work, strive to depict the nobility and greatness I sense, then send it out, hoping someone will recognize that it's good enough to be broadcast to the world. Yes, I want the recognition, but I believe I am longing for something more—a connection to something beyond me that is indeed great. Every now and then I get a glimpse of it, as that audience did when Paul Potts sang. I respond to it, I stand to my feet and applaud it, and I weep because I so long for it.

That audience will remember Mr. Potts' performance, but I believe it will only serve to intensify the longing in them. As a writer, I may sometimes receive recognition, but it will be swiftly gone and the longing will remain. I know only a relationship with God will satisfy it, only striving to be like Him and glorify Him, will fulfill it.

I also know the longing will never completely go away until I am face to face with my Lord. When I connect with the One who put that longing in my heart and serve Him by acting according to His plan for my life, there is a joy and fulfillment that can come from no other source. I will always have that longing in my heart, because I am a child of God, yet separated from Him and therefore not quite whole yet.

My encouragement comes from walking the path He has laid out for me and feeling His presence with me. My joy comes from striving to articulate that longing and His greatness. My hope lies in the reality that one day we will be reunited, and the longing at last will be satisfied.

Chapter 9

After pastoring in that small Alberta church for about seven years, my husband began to feel the tell-tale signs of burn-out. He felt that his creativity was waning, and he was not serving the church as well as he should. A friend suggested a sabbatical might be a good idea. We prayed, and Spence approached the church board with the proposal that we take a leave without pay for one year. When the board agreed, we signed on with Wycliffe Bible Translators and made plans to go to Papua New Guinea, an island in the South Pacific just off the coast of Australia.

It took a few months to jump through all the Wycliffe hoops and when we told the administrative assistant assigned to us that we now had only six months to raise the support we needed, she laughed at us. "This will take two years, possibly more," she said. I could hear the BOHO laughing again, telling me there was no possible way our plans could ever become a reality. But Spence shook his head. "If God wants us there, He'll do the impossible."

Raising support for a family of five was a daunting task to contemplate, but once we began visiting churches and sending out prayer letters, we found unexpected joy in it. Our church posted a large thermometer in the foyer. As it climbed, we were humbled to see the Lord at work on our behalf.

Then the deadline loomed for purchasing our tickets. The church took a special offering for us the Sunday before they had to be in hand. The offering was $800.00 short. We went home, prayed and looked around our home to try and figure out what we could sell in one night. Then there was a knock on the door. A member of our church who had not been able to attend the service that day was stopping by to ask how the offering went. When we told him about the shortage, he took out his chequebook and supplied the needed funds. We bought the tickets the next day.

But the last $1,000.00 per month on that thermometer still needed to be filled in. We kept praying and, once again, the Lord worked a miracle. Spence had been at a conference north of Edmonton several months previous (before we had made the decision to go on the sabbatical), and was so impressed with the speaker that he asked if he would come to our church and give the same message on prayer. After the service the man noticed the thermometer in the foyer and asked about it. Spence explained and the man nodded. "Well, I might be able to help with that. My company regularly supports missionaries." It was only a few days later when he called to tell us that his company had agreed to supply the $1,000 a month. A short while later we found a renter for our house, and I began packing in earnest.

All the details seemed to be lining up when we got a phone call from the mission that slammed on the brakes. There had been an "incident"at Ukarumpa, the mission compound where we would live in PNG. One of the missionaries had been shot in his own home. The voice on the phone sounded glum. "We won't allow you to leave until things have calmed down." I lay in bed that night, wide awake as fear took hold in my heart and mind. I had assumed the compound would be a safe place. Obviously, it was not. What if my husband was shot while we were there? Was it safe to take our three little girls to such a violent place? The Big Old Hairy Ogre was ranting, "What kind of mother would do such a thing?"

I did not express my fears to Spence, but I began to realize that there was no way I could get on that plane. Shortly after that phone call we got a call from a local church, asking us to come and talk about the mission and our role in PNG. After we did our presentation there the pastor invited the people to join him at the front to lay their hands on us and pray. Several did so, but when that pastor prayed specifically against fear (even though he did not know what was in my heart), the fear suddenly disappeared and did not return. A short time later the mission called again to tell us we were now cleared to go.

So it was, in January of 1996, we found ourselves on our way to Ukarumpa, Papua New Guinea. As we circled the grass airstrip in the middle of the PNG highlands, I remember looking down at the jungle canopy and thinking, *Oh Lord, what have we done?*

But there were many other Canadians living in that remote jungle town and they all knew what we were thinking and feeling. They were a great help to relieve our apprehensions as we settled into our new life. We registered our daughters in school: Meagan in Grade One in the elementary school within the compound, Laura and Katie in the high school, a three kilometre bus ride away. They adapted well and quickly. I knew they were going to be fine when Meagan came home one day after playing with a national neighbour's child and said something to me in Tok Pisin.

I knew this was going to be a year of being stretched and challenged. Once again, another divine appointment was scheduled that was also going to push me into unknown writerly territory. As I sat in the personnel director's office listening to him describe what my husband would be doing for the next year, as the mission's flight coordinator, I wondered where I would fit into this strange new place. Then the director looked at me and asked that very same question. "Well," I stammered. "I ... I'm a writer. Is that any help to you?"

His eyes lit up. "Oh, we've been praying for you!" he said. "We need someone right away, in the non-print media department."

"Non-print? But I just said I'm a writer."

He nodded, handed me a piece of paper with the name of the director of the non-print media department and told me how to find the office. The director was an American from California who had been a Hollywood producer for many years. His big booming voice welcomed me to the group. These were radio and TV technicians, people who produced and dubbed videos, and a few national people who worked in the storefront that sold electronic equipment of all kinds.

My new boss told me my first assignment would be to write short radio scripts about what God was doing through the translators working in the jungles of PNG. Those stories would be translated into several languages, sent to Trans World Radio in Guam, and broadcast throughout the South Pacific. He introduced me to a national pastor, a lovely man who edited what I wrote to make sure it would be understood by the cross-cultural audience. It was a privilege and a thrill and a huge blessing to be relating those stories of what God was doing in that far-away place.

They had a system at Ukarumpa that encouraged those who were in the compound to put their names on a list at the post office to invite the translators for a meal during the first two or three days when they were settling back into the centre after several weeks, or months, living in jungle villages. Since my husband worked at the mission's aviation hangar, he knew who was coming and going and would often call to tell me to put our names on that list. Sitting at our dining room table, listening to the amazing stories of what God was doing in those jungle villages stirred my heart and made my fingers itch to get at my keyboard. Sometimes I would only have time to tap out a sentence or two, but those bits later turned into stories and poems that gave God the glory.

I was also privileged to work with some amazing people of great faith, people like Sino. She worked in the store front in the non-print media department. Each Monday morning we would gather for a time of payer and planning and someone would be asked to give a testimony of what God had done in his or her life. Sino's testimony had me riveted on one of those Monday mornings as she spoke in her soft Tok Pisin (the pidgin language spoken by most of the national people). A few years later it became part of my devotional book, *Spur of the Moment*. This is "Sino's Story":

The walk to the prison was long. Sino started early, before the heat of the day, but going anywhere in the highlands of Papua New Guinea meant a long walk up and a harder walk down. She traveled through two valleys and over two mountains to visit her father and bring the food that kept him alive. Her father was one of the most well known "fight leaders" in Enga province. He had killed hundreds, was one of the fiercest cannibals, until Australian law came to the highlands and the police imprisoned him. It had taken several months of visits before he agreed to see his daughter. When he finally did, Sino was almost sorry she had persisted. He was a miserable man who scowled at her and refused to talk, but he took the food she brought.

Sino continued to visit and kept praying that he would listen and take the gift of Christ's forgiveness too. Eventually he was willing to speak with her when she came, but when she tried to talk about God's love and forgiveness, he became angry. Then one day, Sino thought all the months of traveling and praying might pay off. He listened without shouting at her. But when she stopped talking her father said he would never believe her God could love a man like him. "I am too bad," he said, "I have killed too many people. I have eaten too many. Your God would never accept a man like me. Never talk about this Jesus again." (His BOHO was obviously skilled at lying.)

Sino stopped talking about Jesus but she did not stop praying. She prayed that God would send someone who could break through the misery and pain that kept her father in a prison far more dark than the jail where he lived. She kept making the long trip, always wondering how her father would be when she arrived. Would he be calm, or raging and on the edge of madness? She always approached the door to his cell with a dread that could only be eased by praying. Finally there came a day when she was shocked into a speechless stare. Her father was smiling. In all her life she had never seen him smile. For a moment she wondered if he had gone insane.

Then he embraced her and told her a man had come to the warden of the jail and told him God had sent him to talk to someone there, but he did not know who. The warden allowed him to wander through the prison until he found Sino's father. That man had been a fight leader, the killer of many, and a cannibal. He told Sino's father God had forgiven him because of His great love and mercy. He told him how his life had changed and the joy he now had. Sino's father prayed with the man and accepted Christ. He was released from prison in 1994 and traveled the country telling people how Jesus had changed his life.

The writer of Colossians 1:13-14 says, "For He has rescued us from the dominion of darkness and brought us into the kingdom of the Son he loves, in whom we have redemption, the forgiveness of sins." That is the truth that changed Sino's father. It will change anyone who puts his faith in Jesus.

I consider it an honour to be able to write stories like Sino's, stories that tell of God's amazing grace and mercy.

I remember making the trek down the mountain to the non-print media office. The air was fresh and laced with all the floral scents I was slowly becoming accustomed to. Shrouds of spider webs gleamed with morning dew in the tall eucalyptus trees. Bird calls rang all around me. I stopped now and then to admire a vibrantly coloured butterfly. As I approached the market area I heard a man's booming voice and stopped. I had been warned to avoid any assembly that looked threatening. But then I smiled. The market would not open until God's word was preached. I tried to follow the Tok Pisin words as I continued walking, using my ever-present umbrella as a walking stick. I would need to open it on the walk home, when the tropical sun would beat down more intensely. When I reached the grocery store, where we were slowly becoming familiar with the Australian brands interspersed with a few from America, another voice boomed out through the louvered windows and my smile broadened. Hetrik, who led worship at the lotu (church) where we attended, was singing with the other men stocking the shelves before the doors opened for business. I hummed along with the Tok Pisin chorus.

"*Moning nau* [morning now]," Sino greeted me as I stepped into the office. We joined the others for the regular gathering time. I felt the presence of God as we prayed.

When it was over, my boss called me into his office and said they had been tasked with producing a video to celebrate Wycliffe's 40th anniversary in PNG. "We need you to write the script," he said, and explained that I'd work with another woman who'd do all the research for me. "Are you up for it?" he asked.

I stammered again and admitted I'd never done anything like this before but was willing to give it a try. After a couple of weeks the other woman was assigned to a different project and I found myself spending hours in the air conditioned archives building, pawing through photos and reading letters and journals written by people who had been there when Wycliffe first began working in the country. Then I began making phone calls all over the world to interview those people as well as others who were still living at Wycliffe's centre, Ukarumpa. It was an inspiring project, one which grew my faith as well as my writing skills. I learned a lot and worked diligently at the project in spite of being debilitated by a strange condition that gave me extreme vertigo.

It hit suddenly one morning when I got out of bed and stumbled. The room felt like a large platform balanced on a rubber ball. Every time I took a step I had to reach for the wall to regain my balance. By the end of that day I wasn't able to walk at all. I could move my eyes, but if I moved my whole head the vertigo was so extreme I would immediately vomit. The mission's doctor prescribed medication that made me sleep. When the symptoms faded in a couple of days, he reduced the dosage, and I was able to function almost normally.

Later, blood tests revealed no serious illness and I stopped taking the medication. I was greatly relieved to return to the work of writing the video script and get back to a normal routine. But a few days later I again noticed a slight vertigo. By the next day I was unable to function. The "spell," as I called it, lasted for about three days, then I would return to normal. The doctor gave a possible diagnosis: "This could be just a virus, (there were many on that tropical island) and if it is, it will eventually go away," he said, "but if the symptoms persist, you may have what's called Meniere's Disease. There is no cure for it."

When the third bout came, I was crushed. I wondered why on earth God would send me halfway across the world only to paralyze me. I was sure He had put me on the mission field to be productive, as a writer. I wanted to be productive. I had to be productive! But all I could do was weep tears of frustration on those days when even making my way to a chair in our living room was a major effort. After two months of praying, with no change, I realized I would have to face the fact this might be the pattern of my life: three or four days of being absolutely still, then three or four days of being able to write, take care of my family and participate in all the regular routines of life in Ukarumpa.

Feelings of guilt piled up. Everyone else around me was working hard, many of them doing double duty and more, because of lack of staff, and here I was sitting in a chair staring out the window. I felt like a failure. The BOHO told me I should pack my bags and go home. "They'd be better off without you. You're useless, just a burden." I believed it and depression began to sink in.

The third month of "spells" was almost over when, as the vertigo began to wane in its three-day cycle, I decided to go out and sit on the deck at the side of the house. It was a typical PNG morning, bright and sunny, the crisp mountain air full of floral perfumes common in tropical countries. Flowers surrounded the house—hibiscus with huge, vibrant blossoms, bougainvillea, showering the roof of the deck with chartreuse, and the ever-present hedges of scarlet poinsettias.

The woman who owned the house where we lived had planted several rose bushes as well. Using a rake for balance, I walked the edge of the garden, admiring the colors and fragrances. One of the rose bushes caught my eye. A new bud had just blossomed. I stepped close and was enthralled. The bloom was perfectly formed, with dewdrops still glistening on the petals—picture perfect. It was one of those rare moments when the world faded as my focus was captured by the exquisite pattern of God's design. I found myself weeping, not in frustration, as I had so often in the past weeks, but with awe and wonder and praise.

As I gazed at the flower, another Whisperer spoke: "Let me love you for who you are, not what you do." The profound depth of God's love took me completely by surprise as joy welled up at the thought—this rose is complete and beautiful just because it *is*, not because it *does*. All the guilt, anger and frustration were gone. I was free to simply *be*. I was free to allow God's light to shine through me and make me into the beautiful creature he designed, even if that creature could do nothing but sit in a chair and stare out the window. I was loved, even if I couldn't produce anything, even if I couldn't write.

Chapter 10

As I thought back to the time when God overwhelmed me with the reality of the conception of our first child, I rejoiced that the process was still ongoing. He was continuing to teach me about Himself and about my identity—an identity rooted in Him, not in what I could do for Him, not even in my writing. Eventually, the vertigo vanished, the video script was written and produced, and God got the glory.

For many years, indeed, for as long as I can remember, my identity has been totally and inextricably bound up in being a writer. I often told myself, *It's not just what I do, it's who I am*. Sadly, over the years, that perception led me to a place that was filled with stress and burden. In fact, it became like a prison in a way, a prison of my own making.

Eventually I came to a place where I declared that no, indeed, *I am not just a writer*. Every time those words enter my consciousness, even now, I feel the chains fall away. I don't have to produce. I don't have to publish. I don't have to 'succeed' in that way. It is not the essential core of my identity.

I am, in fact, a daughter of my Father in heaven, the King of this universe who demands nothing of me but that I accept His forgiveness, return His love, and let that love flow through me to others. For "now these three remain: faith, hope and love. But the greatest of these is love" (1 Corinthians 13:13, NIV).

I believe God has given me the task of writing as a means to express that truth, to spread that love. He has given it to me as a way to discover more and more about Him for myself. But writing is what I do, not who I am.

It's all a matter of perspective. When my perspective is correct, I am free to be who I was meant to be and then to do what I was meant to do with joy and a sense of freedom. When my perspective is not correct, what I do becomes a chore—I worry about marketing and sales instead of praying for the hearts and minds of my readers, I fear not being able to produce the work I should (the blank page terrifies me). When someone points out a mistake in a published piece I feel humiliated, when my work is rejected I become depressed, when I don't win a contest or an award I become angry and cynical. The Big Old Hairy Ogre racks up multiple points.

I admit—all of these things have happened to me. I knew these feelings were wrong; I struggled against them, but I couldn't deny they were real. All of it began to crush my creativity. It became a struggle to produce. The joy was bleeding away. The ogre was winning.

So, it may seem like a counterproductive thing to do, but I have committed myself to declaring this statement to myself every morning when I sit down at my computer:

I am not just a writer.
I am the daughter of my Father in Heaven.
Nothing else matters. Not even my writing.

When those words sink deep into my soul, then, and only then, will I be adequately prepared to write.

But I am a cracked pot and I do leak. There have been times when I've been stressed, fearing falling behind with my current work in progress or meeting a looming deadline. I don't like the feeling. I get a knot in my stomach and my shoulders tense. I keep telling myself to relax but the "have to" blocks all my creative juices.

There have been times when I have gotten this way in my spiritual life too. I wanted to be a disciplined person—one who adheres strictly to a devotional time, memorizes verses on a regular basis, and remembers to pray for each and every prayer request I heard about.

Sadly, that's not me. As in my writing life, I tend to be more of a "take it as it comes" kind of person. I do write every day, and I do pray every day, but those times are not necessarily scheduled and regular. I've tried to adhere to a strict schedule, but it puts that knot in my stomach. The "have to" dries up my soul.

I used to fret over that, especially as a brand new pastor's wife. Others around me seemed to have a more disciplined life. I set my own bar rather high and almost broke my neck trying to reach it. Until the day God taught me a lesson in a potato patch.

A friend had planted too many potatoes and asked if I would come with my family and dig some up. I did not garden (another failing, I thought, in a church full of gardeners), so I was pleased to say yes. It was a lovely fall day, crisp air, bright sunshine—perfect for a family outing in the country. We had a hoot digging those potatoes. My friend was overjoyed. "I'm so glad you could do this for me," she said, "and it's been a blessing to watch you and your family enjoy yourselves."

On the way home I had an epiphany. Because I didn't garden, my friend had the blessing of generosity and the joy of watching my family have fun. I don't have to be a gardener. I don't have to be just like that other pastor's wife. I don't even have to write 2,000 words a day. God allows me to be just who I am.

Yes, I may get behind in my work in progress from time to time or miss a deadline by a day or two, and I may miss my morning devotions now and then, but when I am there, doing it, the words flow and my spirit is lightened. I feel the joy of doing what I know God intends. I feel the release of being the person He created me to be.

And somehow I've managed to write a few novels, four devotional books and hundreds of articles, some of which God has used to change lives. So when I get a little tense about falling behind I think of that day in the potato patch and I tell myself to breathe.

Then I read one of my favourite scriptures: "Walk with me and work with me—watch how I do it. Learn the unforced rhythms of grace. I won't lay anything heavy or ill-fitting on you. Keep company with me and you'll learn to live freely and lightly" (Matthew 11: 28-30, MSG).

I once wandered in a tired daze at Canada's largest book fair held in a large hotel in Toronto, Canada, staring at thousands of books lined up on the tables. The aisles seemed to go on forever. I felt overwhelmed and despaired of ever making a mark there. As my first book was about to launch into the Canadian Christian marketplace, I realized what a small pond that is.

I'm a firm believer in the significance of the unobtrusive, the power in the hidden talents that appear like the blinking of a firefly—briefly, but so beautifully lighting our world. In the grand scheme of things even the classics, even those on the best seller lists, are brief candles.

But too often I've listened to the "experts," the platform gurus and those making the 'six figure' incomes, telling me to think big. "Get your book on the New York Times Best Sellers list," "Get endorsements from celebrities," "Get on the top TV programs." It seems they are saying that if I don't have a platform of millions of contacts, I have no value as a writer/speaker/minister.

But what if that's not what God has in mind? What if He wants me to keep swimming in my small pond?

The man and woman who guided my husband and I into a relationship with Jesus laboured in a rough northern town and saw no fruit for their labours for almost ten years. But they stayed in that small and no-so-comfortable pond because they knew God wanted them there. That pastor has gone on to glory, and I know he was welcomed with those wonderful words, "Well done, good and faithful servant! You have been faithful with a few things; I will put you in charge of many things. Come and share your master's happiness" (Matthew 25:21, NIV).

It makes me think of the old adage, "It takes many creeks to feed an ocean." It takes many books, many words, to feed the ocean of God's intent. Not all of them will be best sellers, not all will launch their authors into six figure careers, but all, if they were written in and through and with Jesus Christ, will accomplish His purposes.

That's God's economy and it is so often diametrically opposite to the world's. The world says I have to sell a million books to be a success. God says, *Give the work to me so I can bring this one soul into my kingdom.* One soul, brought into the kingdom. It's enough for our Lord. It ought to be enough for me.

There is much wisdom in keeping this perspective and in keeping things simple. Carrie Fountain said this about becoming a poet: "Just get started. Each morning, make a little progress. Send out a little prayer. Take note of something. Try to be facing in the direction of the surprise" (from an interview with Joy Biles).

I think there's a lot of wisdom in her words, wisdom that pertains not only to poets but to writers of all kinds. I think perhaps I try too hard to become a writer. I agonize over it, set my schedule rigidly, watch my reviews on Amazon, try to do a hundred and one things using social media and all the other marketing ploys. And all the while the art suffers because of the "have to," and all the distractions along the way.

Yes, it is necessary to market my work if I want people to discover it. Yes, it is necessary to learn the skills of my craft. But no, I don't have to work so very hard at it that the joy evaporates, and my ears become deaf to the voice that longs to speak to me through my own words.

I love that simple sentence: "Take note of something." That's what it's about. Take note. Watch for it. Record it. Let it live inside me as I express it. Let it change me. Then give it to others so they too may live it, through my work.

For instance, I included a short devotional in *Spur of the Moment*, using an incident my sister and I often laughed about. After my mom had a stroke, we convinced her to hire someone to clean her house. My sister, popping in the day before the housekeeper was to arrive, found my mom trying to wash the kitchen floor, the mop held in her one good hand. When my sister asked why she was doing that she said, "Well, I can't let her see how dirty this floor is!"

I realized that I had been doing the same thing in my relationship with God. So I used the story to illustrate how we often feel about letting God into our lives. We don't want Him to know what a mess we are in, so we don't give Him access. Jesus already knows about the mess and when we allow Him in, He is the one who cleans it up and makes us presentable to His Father.

Sometime after that book was published, I received a letter from a mom who was very concerned about her grown son who had told her he'd "given up on trying to be a Christian." She gave him a copy of *Spur of the*

Moment and was quite surprised when he agreed to read it. She said he told her the short stories were "just right, just enough for me to handle." He said they made sense to him, especially the one about preparing for the housekeeper. "I've been thinking the same way," he said, "shutting the door, afraid that 'the housekeeper' would be offended by the mess inside."

His mom was amazed when he told her that, after reading the scripture attached to the stories, he finds it in his Bible and reads the whole chapter. Her last sentence touched me deeply: "I thought you might like to hear that one wandering young man is being helped to find his way back to God by the very words you wrote!" Soli Deo Gloria!

Yes, "take note of something. Try to be facing in the direction of the surprise." And don't forget to "send out a little prayer."

Chapter 11

Another pivotal moment in my writing career happened one day after we'd come home from Papua New Guinea. I was not very happy about returning to Canada, or rather, specifically, returning to my role as a pastor's wife. I had gotten used to being just another missionary like everyone else at Ukarumpa. Coming back to the "fish bowl," where I felt judged and criticized at every turn, was not easy. Coming back to a "family" who did not seem to understand that the calling to write was from God, after living in a place where it was not only understood but applauded, was almost too much to bear. To keep from being miserable, or from slipping into depression, I began writing a fantasy novel and became, as usual, totally engrossed in the process. Then this happened:

I heard the back door open and close but did not move from my chair in front of my computer desk. I heard my daughter drop her backpack in the hallway and walk into the room. I still did not look up.

Her words began to spill out as she told me that she'd been hurt that day at school. I gave her cursory *uh-huhs*, but kept my eyes on the monitor.

Laura stopped talking. I sensed her turning away but she stopped and burst into tears. "Why do you never have time for me?"

That stab to my heart finally jolted me out of the fantasy I was writing. I sat her down on the couch and we had a good talk. But afterward I realized that something was not right. So I prayed and God responded. We were invited to a pastor's conference soon after—one not within our association and not one we would ordinarily have attended. It became obvious fairly quickly that we were there so that God could get my attention. I resisted most of what He was trying to say to me.

As the conference came to a close, one of the leaders stepped to the front and said he had a word or two from God for some of us. I was more than a bit skeptical. I had seen this kind of thing abused in the past. But the pastor did not point any fingers. Nor did he judge or condemn. He simply took out a small piece of paper and read. He was not looking directly at me when he said, "What you are doing is good but your obsession with it is not," but I knew immediately those words were meant for me. I went home and prayed some more and I began to realize that my writing had become an idol in my life.

It was the same old pattern I had developed before I was a believer. Writing had become my way of escape, my refuge from the world, the source for a solution to my desperate need to bolster my fragile sense of self-worth. Instead of going to God, I went to my writing to satisfy all my needs and take away the emptiness I felt.

I realized this was not what God wanted, so I prayed and asked God what I should do about it. I did not like what He said. He told me to stop writing fiction. Of course I balked, I argued, I cried, and I tried to negotiate. But the same words came back to my heart, over and over again. Stop writing fiction. When I finally realized I had to yield to God's will, I asked him—no, I begged him—to take away all the stories that continuously flowed through my brain. I

112

knew if I could not write them down, I'd go mad. For over a year, He did just that. The stories, characters and scenes disappeared. I wrote only devotions and articles through that period of time.

But God still had a plan. One Sunday morning a woman from a local pregnancy care centre spoke at our church. After the service I had a conversation with her about abortion. She made a statement that stuck in my mind and would not go away. She said, "Can you imagine what it would be like for someone to discover that his mother had tried to abort him, but the abortion failed?"

I did imagine, and the character of Alex Donnelly began to take shape. He was a composite of many people I knew in the Yukon—people who were running away from their past and from God, and sometimes from the police. Again, I prayed and asked God if He wanted me to write Alex's story. He showed me that He did, and the peace that came with that answer assured me it was from God. Then He began to open new doors.

I'd been working at a very stressful job in a hospital at that time and I began to think about leaving it, if only to try and keep my high blood pressure under control. That job ended rather suddenly, and I had a hard time finding another until a friend told me about a small craft store in town that was looking for someone part time. The pay wasn't great, compared to what I was used to, but I felt that familiar nudge and took the job.

When the owner showed me around the shop, she told me there would be times when there just wouldn't be anything to do, "so, you know, bring a book or something." There was a computer in the shop and when I asked if I could use it, she said sure.

Over the next twelve months, using a stack of floppy disks, I wrote my first contemporary novel, *One Smooth Stone*, in that little shop. When I began to create the protagonist for that first novel, it became obvious that this book had to be at least partly set in the north, in Dawson City, Yukon. Since I had lived in Dawson for about twelve years, I had a lot of experience to draw from, and a lot of memories to mine. I could describe what it would be like to live on the Yukon River because I had lived there. I could capture the essence of a minus 60 degrees Celsius day because I'd been in it. But as I wrote the story, I also realized that I had to do some research. It had been a while since I'd lived in the north, so there were some details I had to check. God began to lead me to the people and resources I needed.

At one point in the story, one of the characters uses a cell phone to contact the protagonist, whose only tool for communicating is a radio phone. I was well acquainted with radio phones since that was the only way we communicated to the outside world from our cabin in the bush. But I sat bolt upright in bed one night with the sudden realization that cell phones weren't common when I lived there. Was it even possible to use a cell phone to connect to a radio phone? As I settled back under my covers I made a mental list of who I should call to find out. It turned out to be quite easy—I called a Yukon operator and asked her. She was excited to help an author and gave me all the information I needed.

I also came to a point in the story where I needed to know about some police procedures. The protagonist was in the hospital, but he had also just been arrested. What would that look like? Would he be handcuffed to the hospital bed? Would there be an RCMP constable stationed at the door to his room? I pondered these and other details and remembered a man I had met at a writer's conference who was a ballistics specialist with the RCMP. I pawed through my contact list and was able to get in touch with him. Again, he was more than happy to give me all the information I needed, as well as a few more details I didn't know I needed to know.

My research wasn't just about the Yukon as I wrote *One Smooth Stone*. My characters wandered from there to Vancouver, BC, and then to Seattle, Washington. Since the story arc involved adoption procedures, I had to find out what the policies were in those various places. The rules were quite different from place to place, even from province to province, so I had to go back and adjust the story accordingly.

Writing about the Yukon posed no problem for me as far as describing the setting, but when my publisher wanted part of the story set in the U.S., I had to choose a city and then research it to make that setting just as authentic. I found a couple of good books about Seattle and then mined the internet by reaching out to some of my American friends. A couple had lived in Seattle and were quite willing to read those portions of the novel and make suggestions.

I thoroughly enjoyed the process of writing *One Smooth Stone*. It was thrilling to watch how God directed me to what I needed at just the right time. I hope, at some point in the future, to take a trip back to our old "stomping grounds" so that I can do some research and writing for the third "stone" book *in situ*. There really is no substitute for being there, breathing that air, taking in all those sights and sounds and smells so that it can all be transferred into the story. I've often heard Tolkien's saying, "All who wander are not lost." I would add, "They're just doing research for their next novel!" With more than a little help from above.

The week after I finished that manuscript, the job in that small craft store also ended, and I moved on to another position. I know without a doubt that God gave me that time and place to write that story. I finished it just in time to enter a contest run by The Word Guild and Castle Quay Books, a Christian publisher, both based in Ontario. I mailed it off, with fear and trembling on the very day of the deadline. I asked the woman at the post office to make sure the cancelling date stamp was clear, so the manuscript would not be disqualified.

I tried to forget about the contest, since the winner would not be announced until a few months later at The Word Guild's conference in Guelph, Ontario. That event was just around the corner when I received a phone call from Wendy Nelles, one of the founding members of The Word Guild. She said she noticed that I had not yet registered for the conference. I explained that I had made a trip to Ontario earlier that year, to meet my daughter when she came home from working with a mission group in Bangladesh. I could not afford to pay for another flight as well as the costs for the conference.

Wendy paused, then offered to waive the conference fees. "Do you think you could manage the cost of the flight?" she asked. At first I thought perhaps they needed a teacher at the last minute. Then Wendy said, "You see, your manuscript is the winner of the Best New Canadian Christian Author Award, and we'd really like you to be here to accept it!"

I was stunned. I told Wendy I'd have to discuss it with my husband. I staggered out of my office. Spence frowned and asked me what was wrong. I told him what Wendy had said. "What does that mean?" he asked. I told him it meant my novel was going to be published. "Well then, of course you should go!" he said. Within a short time I found myself in Guelph talking to Larry Willard, owner of Castle Quay Books, about the steps that would be taken to see *One Smooth Stone* in print. I began to pray that the story would be a blessing to those who read it.

When the first box of those books arrived on my doorstep, I gave a copy to a friend who gave it to her daughter, a young woman who had been gang raped when she was a teenager. Understandably, she was bitter and angry with God. But her mom never stopped praying and often gave her books and music that she hoped would bring her back to the Lord. When that young woman looked at *One Smooth Stone*, she thought, *Oh yeah, there goes mom with the God stuff again.* She put it on a shelf in her apartment, never intending to read it. But then she got the flu. And her TV was broken. And she had nothing in her small apartment to read. Except *One Smooth Stone*. She called her mom at midnight, in tears, and said, "I think I finally believe that God still loves me, in spite of everything."

I told my husband I didn't care if I sold any books, it had already accomplished its purpose.

Chapter 12

The writing life is a river of contradictions. Though I have received accolades and wonderful emails about how my words have affected my readers, I've also done a number of book signings where people seemed to go to great lengths to skirt around my little table and avoid eye contact. I've overheard someone talking about my novel, but when her friend asked the author's name she said, "Oh, I don't remember." I've been introduced as an award-winning author, but then had the MC tell the audience that my devotional book was about horses! (Since it's called *Spur of the Moment*, I suppose she should be forgiven.)

Contrary to what many people believe, being an author doesn't really have a lot of celebrity status attached (unless your book happens to land on the New York Times Best Sellers list), and that's just fine with me. It's kind of nice to be anonymous.

I was a bit taken aback when the editor of the newspaper where my faith column appeared asked me to send him a headshot that would be placed with *The Spur*. I wasn't sure I wanted to have that much of a profile in the community, but the editor insisted. And the result was exactly what I had feared would happen, but the fear turned to joy as people began stopping me on the street to talk about something I'd written that week. Sometimes they'd disagree, but often they'd tell me that something in the column had helped them or just made them ponder. I've had emails and letters from people all across the country and beyond, whose lives have been changed by something I wrote.

Some have brought me to tears. Like the email from a friend who gave *Spur of the Moment* to his neighbour. The woman read my piece, "Though My Father Forsake Me," to her husband. He had a daughter from a previous marriage, living in an abusive relationship in a large city in the United States and was moved to contact his daughter and urge her to get out of the situation she was in. She did, returning to her mother's home. My friend thanked me for "a timely reminder of the power and importance of a father's words and love."

And this one from a young woman stationed in Iraq: "I have to deal with the bombs and fighting every day. Just reading this ["Tarnished Mirrors"] made me look outside the box I am in and thank God for every blessing that I have received. Thanks, from a little Texas girl."

Kathleen Gibson, a wonderful writer from Saskatchewan, spoke at the InScribe Fall Conference some time ago. She began her address with these words: "If you have changed a life, you have changed the world."

My head jerked up when I heard that sentence. I'd thought about changing lives before. The emails and letters telling me that God had done exactly that through the words I've put on paper humbled me and encouraged me to keep writing. But changing the world? Really?

Then I thought about another speaker we'd had at one of our conferences. He told us that not very far back in his family line, someone read a book and became a believer in Christ. He told us that now there are many branches to his family, many are preachers of God's word, there are missionaries and others serving in their churches across North America. None of it would have happened but for one book.

I began to consider all the ripple effects that one book has had—not just in the lives of his family members but in all the lives they have touched. I thought about the book I was given just as God was softening my heart toward him. It was a copy of Josh McDowell's *Evidence that Demands a Verdict*. It was put into my hands at exactly the perfect time. It convinced my head that Jesus was who He claimed to be—the Son of God, a man who came to earth to change the world by changing each one of us. I was stunned into awe and gratitude for what the Holy Spirit did in my life through the words in that book.

Words are such small things. They can be simple or profound, plain or eloquent. But when God takes them and bends them to His purposes, He changes hearts with them, and those hearts change the lives of others and those touch others and on and on.

Who knows how far my words will go. If I have changed a life, I have changed the world.

Yes. Really.

It would be all too easy to let such things go to my head, and I confess it has happened a time or two. I have to guard against that continually and remind myself that it isn't my inspirational words that have made a difference in someone's life, but the Spirit of God speaking through those words. He is the only one who can melt a heart and change a life.

He is also the one whose guidance we need to seek. First and foremost. An opposite opinion is often touted in the writing community. I sat at a long table in a writing workshop some time ago and felt like crawling under it as the instructor spoke. I had just realized I was committing what he called the "number one sin of inexperienced freelance writers." I was writing a lot, some of which I thought were fairly good pieces, then

I'd go looking for someone to agree with me and put it all in print. I still had a number of those manuscripts sitting in my "Unpublished" file.

"Write to the market," the instructor suggested. "Find out what's hot and go for it."

This was a new concept for me. The experience is common among new writers, and it follows the path of a common flaw in our human character. We are so self-centred we want to be self-directed. And we forget the One who should be consulted before we even begin.

Too many times I have finished a manuscript and prayed, "Okay God, I've written this (article, novel, short story). Now do your thing."

Not long after sitting in that workshop, I picked up a copy of *Experiencing God* by Henry Blackaby, Richard Blackaby, and Claude King. These words stood out: "God invites you to become involved with Him in His work." I took note of the emphasis. God invites me. I don't invite Him. The work is His, not mine. When I read those words I once again felt like crawling under a table. I realized that I fail all too often to stop and pray before I start tapping away on the keyboard. Too often I don't try to discern what God wants. Too often I do not take the time to look at God's agenda before drawing up my own.

I realized that all of what I wrote should be directed by God and fit within His plan for His kingdom. No matter if it's a personal journal entry or a letter, a feature for a national newspaper, or a book manuscript sent to the number one publishing house in the country, it should be a building block tied to what God is doing in me, in my community, in my country, and perhaps even in the world.

I began to ponder how to discover that and realized the only way was by developing my personal relationship with Him and then keeping my eyes and ears open to see and hear Him. He is here beside me, actively building His kingdom around me. He has invited me to join Him by being one of His scribes in the world.

I pray that I will seek only to find out what's "hot" to Him and go for it. Then I can pray with the psalmist, "May the favor of the Lord our God rest upon us; establish the work of our hands for us, yes, establish the work of our hands" (Psalm 90:17, NIV).

When I first published *Spur of the Moment*, I prayed for that one soul God wanted brought into His kingdom. And, thanks be to God, I was even able to meet her. It was at a speaking engagement at a Christian Women's Club in Alberta. The coordinator touched my arm and pointed. "See that woman at the registration desk?"

I nodded.

"She has been coming to this club for years. She even helps out in various positions, but she's not a believer. We keep praying, but so far ..." She sighed and shrugged.

As I stepped up to the podium that morning I prayed for that woman and was pleased to chat with her for a moment at the book table. I prayed again when she left the room at the end of the event, with a copy of my devotional book, *Spur of the Moment*, in her hand.

A few weeks later the coordinator called me. "I'm so excited! Do you remember the woman I pointed out to you?" When I said yes, she continued. "She asked me to come over for coffee yesterday and she told me she had committed her life to Christ. When I asked her what had finally made her make that decision, she held up your book and said, "This book answered all my questions.""

One soul, brought into the kingdom by a wonderful Saviour, through words written down in obedience. That's God's economy and I am thrilled to be part of it.

But too often, my "economy" rears its ugly head and I start thinking more about how much money I can make from my books, than about how my work can bless those who read it. I was in this frame of mind not long ago when I came across Acts 20:35: "In everything I did, I showed you that by this kind of hard work we must help the weak, remembering the words the Lord Jesus himself said: 'It is more blessed to give than to receive.'"

In his commentary on this passage, J. Hudson Taylor said, "Oh that our pen may be anointed as with fresh oil, while we seek to bring our own soul, and the soul of our readers more fully under the influence of this truth!"

As I search for truth in the world around me, as I strive to depict it, in whatever form, I glorify the One who is truth, the One who lives in me. But there is a danger, the trap of arrogance, the sin of pride. There is danger in loving my words too much, danger in thinking myself wise. I must never assume the words belong to me, neither to keep nor to distribute. The words, especially those that come from the depth of my spirit, belong to my Father. I can never claim divine inspiration, but I must take seriously the calling, the vocation, of a writer who is Christian, to serve my readers, to "bring them under the influence" of truth.

Nor can I claim that I have all the answers. Frans Kafka has said, "One reads in order to ask questions." Perhaps one should also write from that perspective, not to provide, but to seek the answers, those answers that will resonate deep and long as they touch that central part of our being where God resides; those answers that will lead us and our readers to more questions and to a deeper knowledge of God.

The trap of arrogance also lurks, ready to ensnare. It is in arrogance that I write, believing I possess the complete unadulterated truth. Jesus is the only One who lives in that place. Jesus is truth. I am merely one of those, as J. Hudson Taylor says, who is seeking to bring my own soul under its influence.

Oswald Chambers, who has written *My Utmost for His Highest*, one of the most popular devotional books ever written, has said, "The author who benefits you most is not the one who tells you something you did not know before, but the one who gives expression to the truth that has been dumbly struggling in you for utterance."

I think the author who is most true to himself, and his readers, is the one who admits that truth has been dumbly struggling in him or her. It is when I, as a writer, struggle to give utterance, struggle toward that wholeness, that holiness, that I succeed, no matter whether the result is published in the New Yorker or in a local newspaper.

Chapter 13

Anne Rice wrote, "When I'm writing, the darkness is always there. I go where the pain is."

But why do it? Why go to places in my life that are painful? Why put it on the page?

I once attended the First Nations Christian Writers' Conference in Winnipeg Manitoba. The first of its kind in Canada, it was attended by aboriginal people from all over the country. The First Nations Christian Writers' Anthology was launched and several of the authors who had been published in it were there to read.

There was a lot of pain in their stories. A young man wrote about the abuse he suffered in a foster home. A woman wept as she described finding her sister hanging by an electrical cord in a bathroom. Yes, there was a lot to make one shudder. But there was also hope in those stories because they did not stop with the pain, they went beyond it.

Several years ago, I heard Eli Wiesel tell the story about the catalyst that made him write about his experience during the Holocaust. After WW2, he went to Paris to try and find surviving members of his family. He got a job as a journalist and, on one occasion, had to interview Francois Mauriac, the famous Christian writer.

When Mauriac spoke about Jesus, Wiesel exploded and told him to stop. He said that not far from where they were sitting atrocious things had happened to his people. "And we have no words," he said. "We have no words."

Mauriac was deeply moved and responded, "You must find the words. You must write this story." Wiesel began to write, and the result was some of the most powerful work produced about the horrors of that era. Wiesel won the Nobel Prize for *Night*, the writing he put out into the world that we might never forget.

Francois Mauriac was right. I must find the words to express those things that are ugly and evil in order that they cannot defeat me. I must get to the other side of them. This is the writer's acknowledgement of stewardship—the stewardship of my gift and talent. 1 Corinthians 4:2 says, "Now it is required that those who have been given a trust must prove faithful" (NIV). I believe I have been given a trust as a Christian writer and must be faithful to it. To make my life of use to others I must be willing to touch those parts of myself that are universal—those places where the pain lives and the places where the joy of being human has triumphed.

Madeleine L'Engle says in *Walking on Water*, "It is not that what is is not enough, for it is; it is that what is has been disarranged and is crying out to be put in place."

Some people seem to have an underlying belief that writing about what is painful and ugly in life is somehow denying the goodness of God. I disagree. We do not write about the ugly, the dark things, in order to glorify them, nor to question God, but in order to put them in their place and to recognize that there is something more, there is redemption, because of what happened on a cross at the base of a hill in a tiny country then called Palestine.

Bruce Cockburn, the Canadian songwriter and poet, said it well in his song, "Lovers in a Dangerous Time"— "Got to kick at the darkness till it bleeds daylight."

Psalm 12:6 says, "The words of the Lord are pure words: as silver tried in a furnace of earth, purified seven times" (KJV).

"Tried in a furnace of earth." That doesn't sound pleasant to me. "Purified seven times." That sounds like struggle and anguish and pain that has been *forged* into what is pure and wholesome.

As a pottery student many years ago, I learned that you can't use just any old clay to make pottery. It has to be the right consistency, the right combination of elements. Some clay is too fine. When it's thrown on a wheel it won't stand up, won't survive the heat of the kiln, so a substance called grog is added. Grog is clay that has been previously fired in the kiln, then ground into fine particles. Grog sometimes hurts. As you throw a pot on the wheel you can feel it scraping your hands. Sometimes it even makes them bleed.

Good writing needs grog—that stuff that has been ground up inside us as we struggle. We must put the stuff of real life into it or it won't hold up. It won't do what it is intended to do. I wrote this short piece for a local paper some time ago. I called it "Hard Questions":

It seemed fitting that the sky hung heavy and low. It seemed right that the wind was bitter, howling with the fierce shriek of winter around a tiny country cemetery. There was a very small hole in the ground and a very tiny casket to be put into it. It seemed appropriate that we all stood numbed by the cold of that day.

A friend of mine once wrote a poem about Adam, Eve and God in the Garden of Eden. It was a good poem, well-constructed with a strong rhythm and powerful images. One of those images often comes to mind when bad things happen to good people. It's an image of God curled into a fetal position, weeping.

129

Sometimes we ask hard questions. Why did that baby have to die, God? Why is my friend suffering with a painful cancer? Why are those people in Africa starving? We don't usually get a good answer to those questions. They leave us numb and they leave us wondering if God is there.

But then there is that image and that sound. In my friend's poem God mourned the first disobedience, the first break in His relationship with the creatures He put on the earth.

The picture my friend painted with his words was of a God who cares, a God who feels my pain, a God who mourns with me, especially at the graves of tiny babies.

He is also a God who will answer. He is a God who acted to redeem all that was broken in our world. He is a God who continues to do so. The redemption was accomplished on the cross of Calvary, but it is not yet complete. As the writer of the book of Hebrews said, God "waits for his enemies to be made his footstool, for by one sacrifice he has made perfect forever those who are being made holy" (Hebrews 10:13, NIV).

The process is sometimes painful, but the world will one day be made entirely new, entirely redeemed. The scriptures talk about creation groaning as we wait for that day. The groans do not fall on deaf ears, nor will they remain unanswered forever. One day that tiny baby will rise, whole and perfect as God intended him to be.

God's plan is unfolding. What, then, should we do in those times when we groan and feel there is no answer? Again, scripture tells us "to act justly and to love mercy and to walk humbly with your God" (Micah 6:8, NIV).

Humility before God bows the knee and continues to believe. Humility before God acknowledges His sovereignty and calls Him good. Even when babies die and the pain of this world overwhelms, humility before God says, "Blessed be the name of the Lord."

The Sunday after that piece appeared in print, the father of that baby approached me in the lobby of our church. He said he was in a local restaurant when he read "Hard Questions." I held my breath as he described what he felt. He said it wasn't long before tears were streaming down his face. Many things flew through my mind. Was he angry with me? Should I have written and published that piece when it exposed not only my pain, but his?

Then, with tears brimming in his eyes he said, "Thank you. It was part of the healing. Thank you for writing it. Thank you for putting it in a place where I could read it."

Madeleine L'Engle says, "The discipline of creation, be it to paint, compose, write, is an effort toward wholeness" (*Walking on Water*). This is the responsibility—to struggle toward that wholeness in my life and in my work, to take my work deeper, to make sure it has enough "grog" in it to stand, and perhaps even to help with the healing. All to the glory of God, because that is His plan for my work.

Writing coach Natalie Goldberg wrote in *Wild Mind*, "A writer must be willing to sit at the bottom of the pit, commit herself to stay there, and let all the wild animals approach, even call them up, then face them, write them down, and not run away."

My daughter Kate once told us about an adventure her friend had while traveling in Africa. The young woman sat cross-legged on the ground, surrounded by tall grass. She had been told to sit very still. She could hear snuffling noises and now and then a grunt. When the massive head of a gorilla poked out between the grasses, she was tempted to leap up and run. But she forced herself to sit quietly. The gorilla approached, moved around her, touched her hair, sniffed her shoulder. She remembered the instructions she was given: "No sudden movements. Keep your eyes on the ground." She tried not to think of what those massive hands and arms could do to her. She tried to relax her shoulders. Slowly. Another gorilla approached, then another. They investigated her, sat close by grooming one another before slowly ambling away. That young woman said she let out her breath and smiled. "I'd just won a great victory over fear," she said. "I think it was the adrenalin coursing through my body that made me laugh out loud."

Yes. We must let the gorillas come, and we must contend with the dark things. Like dark trees. There seems to be a trend, at least in my community, to line the streets with them. I don't like them. When I drive down a street where a string of these trees have been planted, I turn away. They seem unnatural to me. They remind me of horror movies in which innocent young women are running through tangled woods trying to evade a crazed murderer.

But one day, as I glanced out my window at the tree in my neighbour's yard (yes, it's a dark one), I was so attracted to it I stood up and walked to the window. The slant of light striking the tree made its dark red leaves glow with a crimson hue. It was beautiful and I stood there, transfixed.

As that dark tree turned into something glorious, I thought of God's work in my life. He is in the business of transformation. He transformed me from a bitter angry person into one who is growing in the understanding of the words joy and peace, grace, mercy, and forgiveness. And the red colour of the leaves had a new significance too, in that light, as I thought of the blood of my Saviour, poured out that I might have new life.

As I watched that tree begin to glow I pondered, and I considered Ted Dekker's words, that all good fiction is transformational. Dekker stresses that "you must long for a new way of being in the world to write good story." Those words resonated with me because lately I've been feeling that God is wanting me to go deeper, to seek Him more. Mr. Dekker believes that is the first step to writing transformational fiction, and I agree.

Jesus did indeed teach us a "new way of being in the world." He turned His culture upside down in many ways, turning the people back to the core truths of the scriptures they thought they knew and putting their feet on a straight path that led to His Father. Some responded and were transformed: fishermen became leaders, cowards became brave, unlearned men became teachers, downtrodden women were raised up.

There will always be dark trees in this world, things that make me shiver. The good news is that even those things can be transformed by our God into beacons of light. There will always be dark trees in my own life, things that could prevent me from moving forward in Christ. The good news is that He has given me the ability to overcome those dark things as I move closer to Him. For, as the apostle John has said, "You, dear children, are from God and have overcome them, because the one who is in you is greater than the one who is in the world" (1 John 4:4, NIV).

Chapter 14

Like most writers I am a dreamer. I dream of accolades and awards, and money flowing into my bank account. Sometimes it feels like those dreams are close to coming true. But sometimes my dreams are crushed. My "career" sometimes looks like nothing but a pile of pointless efforts. All the sacrifices seem to have been for nothing and I come close to giving up on all the dreams.

I was mulling on such negative thoughts, when I realized I needed a spiritual perspective, so I opened my Bible and discovered that was the state the disciples were in when Jesus was crucified. The hardest day in their lives was probably the day before the resurrection— that very long day when they were in hiding, fearing that they too might end up on a cross.

I imagined the dreams the disciples had—dreams perhaps of the glory and acclaim they would have as His disciples when they came into their own in His new kingdom. It was an earthly kingdom they were dreaming of that did not include the brutal rule of the Romans.

I imagined what they'd sacrificed—they'd left their homes, families, their livelihoods, the fishing nets that supplied their food; in Matthew's case, the money collection stall that made him wealthy; in Luke's case, a fulfilling and no doubt lucrative medical practice.

They'd allowed Jesus to turn their lives upside down. And now what? He was gone and it looked like it had all been for nothing.

No wonder Peter said, "I'm going fishing" (John 21:3, my paraphrase). He'd given up on the dreams. He didn't know what to do with himself, so he went back to what he knew—casting his nets, and he took some of the other disciples with him.

But then I read further, about what happened next. In the last part of verse 3 of John 21 it says, "but that night they caught nothing." Then, early in the morning, when they were heading back to shore empty handed, a man calls out to them, "Friends, haven't you caught any fish?"

I imagined the tone of their voices when they said no. The stranger tells them to throw their nets on the right side of their boat. And then it happened. The nets were so full they couldn't haul them in and then they recognized the man. Jesus.

I love this next part. Jesus has made a fire and is cooking fish. When the disciples arrive, he says, "Bring some of the fish *you* have caught." I can just imagine their bewilderment as they struggled to understand what Jesus was trying to teach them.

I think he was trying to tell them that he had more for them to do than just catch fish, more for them to be concerned about than just making a living. He was telling them He would provide for them. And He was telling them they would have a role to play in it all. The story wasn't over. In fact, it was just beginning.

Noted author and counsellor, Larry Crabb wrote in *Shattered Dreams*, "God is always working to make His children aware of a dream that remains alive beneath the rubble of every shattered dream, a new dream that when realized will release a new song, sung with tears, till God wipes them away and we sing with nothing but joy in our hearts."

I had a few tears in my eyes as I finished reading. Yes, sometimes my dreams can look like they're dead, but if I lift up my head, Jesus is there, with a better plan, and new dreams for my life and for my work as a Christian writer. He has proven it over and over again.

He proved it through a difficult stretch of time that began on April 1st, 2011, when I received one of those phone calls no one ever wants to receive. I was at a conference at the time, manning my booth with all my books, hoping to have a good day of selling and connecting with potential readers. Then my cell phone rang, and my doctor's voice gave me the bad news. "I'm so sorry to have to tell you this, Marcia, but the tests came back positive for breast cancer."

I wanted to believe it was an April Fool's Day joke, but it wasn't. It was the beginning of a long arduous journey full of chemo and radiation treatments, days when I could hardly move and days when I just wanted to open my eyes and find myself in heaven. I did not write very much during that year, but a friend sent me a link to a website called Caring Bridge. It was a place where I could post updates on my cancer journey for friends and family. It was a way to avoid too many phone calls I did not have the energy to answer. It was also a way to work through the confusion and challenges I faced every day.

Long days, like the one I wrote about on Caring Bridge:

It had been a long grey day in a long grey week. The new chemotherapy drug they had said would be easier, wasn't. It knocked me to the ground, then stomped on me until every bone ached. I was seriously thinking about cancelling the next dose. I just didn't think I could do it.

Then, late one afternoon, as I lay on our living

137

room couch groaning, I opened my eyes. A thin beam of light had pushed through the clouds, through my living room window, and along a slim tendril growing out of a small spider plant. The tendril had looked so fragile as it reached out, pale and oh so thin. But when that beam of light touched it, it began to glow. Then the light illuminated the tiny white flowers that had just bloomed. The flowers glowed in that ethereal light. It took my breath away. And hope blossomed.

Hope. At that moment it was a living dimension. A shaft of real light that slipped into my living room along that tendril of plant at just at the right moment. At just the right moment God reminded me that he was here, watching, waiting with me and smiling as he made that tiny flower glow.

"When Jesus spoke to the people, he said, 'I am the light of the world. Whoever follows me will never walk in darkness but will have the light of life.'" (John 8:12).

The light of life, the light of hope. It's Him. Jesus Himself. Right here. Right now.

Yes, even in the midst of a dark place like living with cancer, God proved his love and showed me that I am held in the palm of his hand. He gave me a heart more open to compassion and words to express my confusion and pain. He let me know that my dreams were not dead but had been channeled into paths that grew my faith and my gratitude. His plan for my life and my work became more clear and took me to that place of humility that is so needed to balance my pride. And the depth of His love strengthened my resolve to be faithful to His call on my life, to write.

After I came through that season of struggling with cancer, my husband decided we needed to go on a

138

cruise. It was a great trip, for the most part, but there were some things I found irritating. I often felt we were made to feel that we weren't quite worthy of being on that ship. The BOHO, of course, reinforced that idea.

One day we decided to go to an art auction. If you attended, you were automatically entered into a draw. I was a little excited when I won a gift bag. There was a watch in it that had a rather large price tag on it. That was nice. But then I realized there was also a $100.00 gift certificate included. I'd spotted something I liked in one of the boutiques. With the gift certificate I could easily afford it. So yes, I got a little excited.

Until I read the fine print. The certificate was only good at one of the high-end jewelry shops. It didn't take long for all of us to realize that I was not going to be using that gift certificate in that shop. By the time I left, the well-dressed clerk was looking condescendingly down his nose at me. I felt a little like I'd been trying to steal something by the time I left.

Then I had a closer look at the watch. It had scratches on the buckle and a stain on the wrist band. I know they say you shouldn't look a gift horse in the mouth, and I really did try to be thankful, but I confess it left me with a bad taste in my mouth, especially when I later saw it "on sale" for $24.95! It felt like they were saying I wasn't worthy of receiving something of true value, so, here, take this second-hand tainted bobble and be happy. It wasn't a nice feeling.

Much later, I thought of my experience in terms of my readers. Do I give them something of value, something of true worth? Do I respect my readers? If I give them watches with scratches on the buckle and stains on the wristband, they aren't going to be very happy with me. They probably won't finish the book they started and certainly won't look for any others I've written. My readers want and deserve quality writing, writing without typos and grammatical errors, novels in which the reader is captivated by the characters and swept away by the setting.

Learning to do that takes time and practice. There are no short cuts to producing a work of true value. I owe it to my readers to take the time and effort to give them something that is truly worth the money and time they will invest in it.

After all, my readers are made in God's image, being groomed for God's eternity. He values them, calls them a "chosen people, a royal priesthood, a holy nation, God's special possession" (1 Peter 2:9, NIV). If God values everyone so highly, should I not also? Should I not always strive to give my best to my readers? I have learned over the years doing so is only possible with God at my side, guiding and directing my words.

Chapter 15

I took a deep breath and tried to stop shaking. The big Paint Horse in front of me was over 17 hands high. I'm just over five feet. I put my hand on his hip and shoved. He side-stepped a bit closer to the box I used to saddle him. The saddle was almost in place when he shifted sideways again, and I fell to the ground with a groan. It took me a few more minutes to get Cheyenne back in place and the saddle firmly cinched around his wide girth.

I took another deep breath, crawled up onto the stack of hay bales I used to mount him, and put my foot in the stirrup. Cheyenne lunged forward. I barely managed to swing my leg over and put my seat down. Once I was settled into the saddle, holding the reins firmly, with only a slight movement of my hands and legs I could easily direct that huge animal. Cheyenne loved to run, and I loved to let him.

I've always been horse crazy. It took many years of begging before my mother let me anywhere near a horse and many more after that before I owned one. I remember the day I woke up and looked out my bedroom window and saw Cheyenne grazing in the field beside our home beside the Klondike River. I almost pinched myself to make sure I wasn't dreaming. I was awestruck, but just seeing him there made me shake. This was a real live horse, who needed to be fed and groomed and cared for in all kinds of ways and he was now my responsibility. But when I was on his back, charging across an open field, I forgot all about the responsibility and just let the thrill of riding course through me.

Sometimes I still shake that way when I begin to work on a new writing project, especially a book. The task is so daunting, so huge, so important. It often leaves me a bit awestruck. I can't help but think of the serious responsibility I have as the keeper of the gift of being a writer of faith, a writer in God's kingdom. But then the keys begin to clack and the words begin to flow and I forget all about the responsibility. I just let the thrill of creating course through me.

I remember watching a blues singer perform on a small stage at the university I attended years ago. The man was a master of his art. He played and sang as though he were controlling a strong animal. He captivated his audience, and he gloried in it. At one point, he started to nod and then he smiled. Then he laughed out loud. It had all come together. The instruments, his voice, the eagerness of the audience. It was one big "Yes!" and he knew it.

Many have quoted that famous line from *Chariots of Fire* where Eric Liddell says, "When I run, I feel His pleasure." Sometimes when I write, I sense His laughter. When I'm in the moment, in Him, tied to Him through the words that are pouring out, it is like nothing else matters. It is one big "Yes!"

I think perhaps this is what Paul meant by "in him it has always been 'Yes'" (2 Corinthians 1:19, NIV)—an emphatic, triumphant, laugh in the face of evil, shouted from the rooftops, "Yes!"

When we are in Christ, doing what He has called us to do, loving Him and loving the work, it will always be a joyous "Yes!"

I have had that same feeling of sensing God's pleasure and approval when teaching. I was once

142

asked to speak about poetry to a group of students in a Christian school. The group would include grades four to eight. As I planned, I prayed that the Lord would give me words and stories to engage all the students, despite such a big range in age.

When I walked into the classroom the younger students sat in front, older in back. A row of grade eight boys stood along the back wall, all of them with their arms crossed over their chests. I read their body language immediately: "No old woman is going to get me interested in poetry."

I had intended to end my talk with a story about Irina Ratushinskaya, the Russian dissident imprisoned for her work. But I immediately adapted and began with that story.

"You may think poetry has no power." I spoke directly to those boys in the back. "But let me tell you a story." They leaned forward as I told them how this brave woman wrote her poetry in soap while in prison, memorizing over 250 poems in the hope that one day they would be read. I told them that Ms. Ratushinskaya was deprived of Russian citizenship. "Why do you think they did that?" I asked those boys, giving them a moment to ponder before answering the question myself. "Because they were afraid— afraid of a poet's words." By the end of that class, it was thrilling to see those students get excited about writing poetry. Some of the best poems were written by those older boys.

God had guided and directed me in that classroom. He led me to adapt.

Dictionary.com lists two verbs under the word adapt. The first verb is used with an object, such as, "I adapt my work to my audience." The second verb is used without an object, such as "I adapt."

Sometimes the two go hand in hand.

When I walked into that classroom, I knew that adapting to my audience was a matter of survival—it was crucial to being heard.

Adapting my writing to any audience is the same. The first time I submitted a short story to a Sunday School publication, the publisher said she loved the story, but it was too long for their readers. "Cut it in half," she advised. I groaned but did as she asked and it was published. Adapting is a matter of survival.

Adapting to my audience in prayer is the same. I often come before God with a long list of requests. Help this one, do that for that one, give me the desires in my heart. But if I truly come into God's presence, I find I must adapt myself, I must bow humbly before Him, draw close, and listen to the One who is my one true audience.

I must also learn to adapt my life to His way of acting in the world, His way of seeing the world. As I do so I begin not only to survive as a follower of Christ, but to thrive. The writing then flows from a place of strength, not weakness, because it flows from a heart that has been changed, a soul that is the home of His Holy Spirit.

Chapter 16

There have been times when God has reminded me of what this "writing game" is really all about.

I didn't participate in a lot of track and field events when I was young. The high school I attended did not have the resources for much. But we did have a relay team and I have often been inspired by the things our coach taught us as we were training and competing.

"Stop thinking of yourself as a single unit." Our coach leaned forward, her voice raised above the cheering of the crowds, her eyes flicking from one girl to the next. "It's all about the team," she said. "When that baton leaves your hand your job is to cheer your teammate on."

Right. That's what it was all about. We were on a relay team and the point was to get that baton into our teammates' hands so they could run with it all the way to the finish line.

I thought of that day long ago, when I read the words in Habakkuk 2:2, "Write the vision and make it plain on tablets, that he may run who reads it" (NKJV).

It came to mind again a while ago when I received a message from someone thanking me for something I'd written. Usually, I make a point of asking where they read the piece, and sometimes, as on this day, I'm surprised. The woman told me a friend had seen it on someone's website, copied it, and sent it to her by email. This wasn't the first time that had happened. The world wide web is just that and the words we put out there are sometimes spread around without our knowledge nor consent. That used to bother me. My work is copyrighted—no one has the right to just grab it and run with it.

Then I remembered my coach's words and the words God spoke to Habakkuk. It felt like God was tapping me on my shoulder.

Oh. Right. That's what this is all about, really. I'm writing so that others will take my words to heart and then share them with others. The words aren't meant to be just pretty decorations on a page that will bring me satisfaction and praise. They are meant to help others, to change lives, to draw people closer to the One who inspired them. I want my readers to "run" with my words—to live a life of joy in service to the Lord and to pass that on to those around them so they can run with them too, all the way to the finish line.

So now, when someone emails to tell me they've read my work on someone's website or blog or in an email, I cheer them on. I'm glad they're running with it. Because that's what it's all about.

Poet Mary Oliver wrote in her poem, "Sometimes":

> Instructions for living a life:
> *Pay attention.*
> *Be astonished*
> *Tell about it.*

Sounds like good advice for living a writing life. It's a writer's job to observe, to step back from the moment and ponder what might be happening, what might be important, what might be worthy of being recorded.

I love this excerpt from Elizabeth Barrett Browning's *Aurora Leigh*—

Earth's crammed with heaven,
And every common bush afire with God;
But only he who sees takes off his shoes,
The rest sit round it and pluck blackberries,
And daub their natural faces unaware.

I've had many moments in my life when I've taken note—watching others watch life as it happened. I remember watching my two-year-old nephew's eyes widen with wonder when I turned his head so he could see an iris that had just bloomed. I remember seeing the light in my mother-in-law's eyes when her son showed up unexpectedly with a bouquet of flowers in his hand. I remember learning what the word cherish meant as I watched a man who thought he'd never have a child shower his daughter with affection. I have written about all of those moments, moments in time when I paid attention, when I "took off my shoes," as Ms. Browning encourages us all to do in her wonderful poem, and was astonished, and went on to tell about it. Those moments were gifts from the hand of God.

Like all gifts, those God gives me through my talent and skill as a writer are meant to be signposts pointing to Jesus. As the Hebrew people learned, when they entered the promised land, a moment in time that was recorded for us in Joshua chapter 4. God instructed the people to take stones from the river and construct a memorial, not just to mark the moment, but to turn the heads and hearts of present and future generations toward Him in all his goodness, power and glory.

As a writer of faith, I am, in a sense, the bearer of such stones of remembrance. My task is to build words into stories like stones piled up into altars and memorials. It is up to me to write the words that point to the beauty in our world, words that turn heads so they will look and see the true character of God, words

147

that cry out for mercy and justice when what lies before me is corrupt and unjust.

And as I place these stones carefully and deliberately, I too am blessed because they aren't just stones, they aren't just words. They are holy instruments of God.

"Each of you is to take up a stone on his shoulder ... to serve as a sign among you ... these stones are to be a memorial to the people of Israel forever" (Joshua 4:5-7, NIV).

But sometimes, I forget my purpose. I am susceptible to distractions that are just too hard to ignore. Picture this: a young woman stands at the head of a long runway, a wooden baton in her hand. At her side sits an eager German Shepherd. He is looking up at her, quivering. The woman swings the baton in front of the dog's nose, then pitches it to the far end of the runway. The dog shoots down the runway, ignoring the bowls of food and snacks laid out along its sides, grabs the baton and races back to his mistress. He drops the baton at her feet and sits down. He looks very pleased with himself. Really. He does.

Another young woman takes her place at the head of the runway. The bowls of food and treats are still in place. A Golden Retriever sits at her side. He looks around and wags his tail. The baton is waved and tossed. The Retriever heads off, but spots a bowl of food and grabs a bite. He gets a bit further, but that bowl of treats is just too tempting. A few more steps but oh, there's another bowl of fragrant food just made for him. At the halfway point the dog is so distracted he ends up turned around and heading the wrong way.

I laughed out loud the first time I saw that video. We owned two Golden Retrievers at the time, and I knew that's exactly how they would perform if given the chance.

And it's a lot like how I perform at times. Distractions abound and sometimes I just can't resist. There's that internet expert promising a six-figure income if I just follow her plan. There's another guy who says he can help build my platform so that even Oprah will want to interview me. And ooh, there's a course that teaches everything I need to know about building a website, creating social media banners, and all kinds of wonderfully creative things every writer absolutely needs.

I got caught by a distraction recently that I am now regretting. It sounded so good, a way to finally make some money, at least enough to keep publishing without the stress of worrying if my latest project is going to break even. Once I started the course, I realized it was going to take a lot more time and effort than I expected. The days flew by with little writing getting done because I was chasing after the bowls filled with dreams and promises. And suddenly, like that golden retriever, I ended up going the wrong way altogether.

It's then I had to stop and ask myself, okay, what is the right way? How can I get down that runway to the goal God has assigned me? It's then I had to remember what my calling is all about—those stones of remembrance—and connect again with the One who designed it for me. I want to be like that German Shepherd, eager to please my Master and running with all I have, to do what He wants me to do. I want to focus on the true prize, not a reward, not a treat that will be devoured in seconds, but a life-giving relationship. I want to invest in that which is eternal.

So, "I press on toward the goal to win the prize for which God has called me heavenward in Christ Jesus" (Philippians 3:14, NIV).

Many times, God has given me what I need to do just that. I don't remember how I heard about it, but I know God brought it to my attention and when I looked up the School of Writing at Canadian Mennonite University in Winnipeg, I was thrilled to discover that one of my literary heroes, and Canadian literary icon, Rudy Wiebe, was accepting applications into the Advanced Fiction Mentorship Program.

I was about halfway through writing *A Tumbled Stone*, the sequel to *One Smooth Stone*, and I wondered, would my writing be good enough to be accepted into that mentorship program? *One Smooth Stone* had gotten some good reviews from the Christian publishing world, but how would my work hold up in the established literary world?

I sat down and filled out the application, selecting three short stories to submit, as required. And heard nothing back. No email, no phone call. I was disappointed but not really surprised. My self-doubt and the ever-present imposter syndrome kicked in. The Big Old Hairy Ogre mocked. "Of course you weren't accepted—you know you're not in that league."

Then I received a large manilla envelope in the mail. When I saw the return address was the Mennonite university I thought, *Oh great, now I'm on their mailing list. It's probably their school calendar.* The envelope sat on our coffee table for several days. I was tidying up the living room one afternoon and almost tossed it into the garbage, but decided I'd have a look, just out of curiosity. I was stunned to find a letter of acceptance to the mentorship program. I had one day to let them know if I was going to attend. I picked up the phone and called to tell them yes and I thanked God that I had not thrown that envelope away.

A short time later I found myself packing. I sorted my belongings, leaving behind anything I thought I would not need for that week in Winnipeg. I decided to take only a small purse and one credit card. I would not be driving so I left my driver's license in my wallet. My husband dropped me off at the Edmonton airport and I made my way to the long line progressing slowly towards the counter where I would pick up my ticket.

As I stood there, I noticed two men bearing two long cases who were in conversation with an airline official. I watched as they opened the cases to reveal their rifles and filled out a lot of paperwork. They walked away and the airline official glanced up at me. "Where are you off to, ma'am?" he asked. When I told him Winnipeg he waved me over. "I'll check you in here," he said, and tapped on the computer. I was delighted to be avoiding the long line and thanked the Lord. "Here we go,"the attendant said. "Just need your photo ID and you're all set."

My heart sank. Photo ID! Like a driver's license, which was sitting in my wallet at home.

"How about a Costco card?"

I shook my head.

"Anything with a photo of you on it?"

I almost burst into tears. I knew there wasn't time to have my husband bring it to me.

The attendant looked sympathetic. "Do you have a fax machine in your house? Is there someone who could send us a copy of your driver's license?"

I tried to slow my heartbeat. "Yes! My daughter can do that."

He gave me the number and I called Meagan and walked her through the process. The attendant told me to stay there while he went up to the airline's offices. He returned in a few minutes with the copy of my license and explained which security line to go to. "They know you're coming so just give them this piece of paper."Then he warned me that I would probably not be able to do this again on the way back, so I needed to have the license sent to me in Winnipeg before the return flight.

I thanked him profusely and was greatly relieved to get through security easily and into the departure lounge before the boarding announcement was made. I was very much aware that God had just worked on my behalf. He'd given me a kind and caring airline attendant who went out of his way to get me on that plane to Winnipeg. I had no doubt Satan had tried to prevent it and it humbled me to know that God, once again, had a plan that He would not allow to be thwarted.

And God had another gift for me, once I was on the plane. As I settled into my seat on the small aircraft, the stewardess came down the aisle and asked us all to move forward, to balance the load. I ended up sitting one seat back and across the aisle from a young woman who took out a book to read. As she did so, the colour caught my eye. Hmm ... same colour as the cover of my novel.

I watched out the window as the ground dropped away and the plane lifted off, then glanced across the aisle again. The young woman had turned the book. My book. It was a surreal moment. A comforting, though in a way, disconcerting moment. What did she think of it? She seemed to be reading eagerly enough. But did she like it? Was it good enough to capture her imagination? For the rest of the flight I peeked over at the woman, trying to gauge her reaction. In the flurry of disembarking, I lost track of her and never did find out. But I felt as though God had just given me a special reassurance.

Then I arrived at the University and was swept into the routine of classes and writing assignments. I was nervous about going to the first session, even though my work had been accepted, because I had chosen to workshop something other than those three short stories—the opening pages of *A Tumbled Stone*. Would Rudy and the other students like it? Would the writing be good enough?

The day my excerpt from *A Tumbled Stone* was to be critiqued, my palms were sweating and my heart was beating a little faster than normal. My fellow classmates began to comment on my work. According to the rules, I was not allowed to speak until Rudy gave me permission. Staying silent was at once a relief and a hardship. Then Rudy made some comments, asking for further input from the class as they dissected the excerpt.

Then his words, "This is good writing." Affirming words from "the master." I could have danced down the aisle. I think I literally floated through the rest of that week.

But the euphoria wore off when I returned home and continued to work on the manuscript. What will people think of it? Will it be good enough? Again, the BOHO said no. It was a struggle to block his taunts.

About that time, I was encouraged to consider why I write and I came to a few conclusions. I write because it's the way I'm "wired." Because I can't not write. Because the images and characters and scenes and emotions flood out of me through a keyboard and I can't stop them, any more than I could stand in a flood and stop the raging waters.

And then I remembered who made me this way, who controls what happens to the words I type on my computer, and who will someday say, "Well done," if I work in obedience to Him.

And I realized how much I want to hear *that* Master's voice and how much I want to someday dance down the aisle that leads to His throne. So I go on, trying to be obedient to the task of being a writer, fighting off the self-doubt and the need for affirmation from men when the only thing that counts is affirmation from Him.

Chapter 17

There's a paragraph on the opening page of my website that says, "It's been said that we are all just walking each other home. That is the theme and goal of my life and my work, that we might all join hands and find the place where we all belong—in the palm of God's hand." I have titled my newsletter, *Words to Take us Home*.

Home is the place we all long for, the place where we can feel safe, the place where we feel seen. I believe much of our lives are spent in that pursuit. There's a cautionary tale about it in the book of Genesis. I've often pondered and marveled at the story of Noah. It's an old story, one taught to children in Sunday School because it's all about obedience.

After the flood, God gave the people who stepped out of the ark a command: "multiply on the earth and increase upon it" (Genesis 9:7, NIV). He wanted them to scatter. But some decided it was better to stay together and build a fortified city and a tower that would reach to the heavens. They decided their plan was superior to God's. They did it to keep themselves safe, perhaps thinking a city and a tower would save them from another flood, even though God had promised never to flood the earth again. And they did it "so that we may make a name for ourselves" (Genesis 11:4b, NIV).

As I read those words, my conscience was pricked just a little. I realized I'm too much like those Babel-builders in wanting to make a name for myself, wanting to be known and seen. With every book I've written I confess I've thought, *maybe this one will make it onto a bestseller list. Maybe this one will make me known.*

In his commentary on Genisis 11, Matthew Henry states,

> These Babel-builders put themselves to a great deal of foolish expense to make themselves a name; but they could not gain even this point, for we do not find in any history the name of so much as one ... Philo Judaeus says, "They engraved, every one, his name upon a brick, *in Perpetua rei memoriam-as a perpetual memorial;* yet neither did this serve their purpose.

Matthew Henry calls the tower of Babel, a "presumptuous, provoking design."

It's a common failing, and a very old one, according to the scriptures. We all want to make a name for ourselves. God's intent is that we make His name known. That's why He told the descendants of Noah to scatter and multiply, so that God's glory would be revealed, His promises remembered, His plan for humanity accomplished.

God foiled the plan of those early inhabitants of the earth by confounding their language. I believe He will foil any of my plans that are not according to His will. He does it because, as Matthew Henry says, "It is just with God to bury those names in the dust which are raised by sin." God's justice prevents the chaos that would result from my impudence and pride. He knows all my failings, my inclinations to foolishness like carving a name in a brick and believing it will last forever.

As I ponder these things my prayer is that I will be obedient to the calling God has put on my heart, that I allow Him to direct not only my work but my life. One more thing Matthew Henry said will stay with me:

What a difference there is between men's building and God's; when men build their Babel, brick and slime are their best materials; but, when God builds his Jerusalem, he lays even the *foundations of it with sapphires, and all its borders with pleasant stones*" (Isaiah 54:11,12; Revelation 21:19).

I believe it is that home that I am indeed longing for, because deep inside I know that it is my true home, the place where I will be truly seen, when I come face to face with Jesus. That longing is valid and good. The longing to win the acclaim of man and bring glory to myself, is not. Lord, save me from presumptuous provoking designs. Help me to keep my eyes on you and the true calling on my life.

I once heard Philip Yancey being interviewed. He was asked what it was like being a famous writer. He told a story of how he sometimes felt guilty when his wife would come home after a busy day of helping people and ask him what he'd done that day. His answer—"Well, I found a great adverb!"—made him feel less than adequate.

I've had those same feelings from time to time, especially when a member of our congregation looked at me like I'm that two-headed writer who sits at a computer all day and doesn't really "do" anything.

A while ago my husband and I were surfing the channels on TV when we happened upon a biography of Henri Nouwen, narrated by Jean Vanier. I was moved by Nouwen's story, by the humility he learned when he went from being an acclaimed professor and author to a caregiver for a mentally challenged, physically incapacitated adult named Adam at L'Arche Daybreak Community in Montreal.

And I was struck by Jean Vanier's words: "Henri's call was not just to be with Adam or just to care for him, it was to announce him to us, to the world."

It's at those times, when I feel the inadequacy Philip Yancey mentioned, or listen to the BOHO and the disapproving words from misguided "saints," that Jean Vanier's words ring with a truth I try not to forget. When I feel misunderstood or even guilty, I remember that there were those in the Bible whose only role was to sit at the king's feet and write down what He did. They were to announce the king's greatness to their world.

I often wonder what it would have been like to be a scribe during the ancient times. What would it have been like to sit in the courts of Xerxes or King Saul and King David? Did those scribes realize the importance of the history they were recording? They were trained to be accurate, to record the very words of their king as though their lives depended on it. Often it did. But did they have moments of awe as they wrote? Perhaps not.

Perhaps it was just a job, a very ordinary thing to sit at the feet of the king and record his words and the everyday goings-on in his court. Perhaps yes. Perhaps a particular ray of light as it hit the king's crown caught the scribe's eye, or the compassion in his master's eye as he listened to the stories of his subjects. Perhaps his heart was moved as he wrote.

I too am a scribe, recording my times, recording and revealing the glory of my King as He reveals it to me. It is my job to lean into it, to recognize its importance, to be moved by it, for the very quality of my life may depend on it; the very direction of a person's life may change because of it. Just as Henri Nouwen announced the beauty of God in the guise of a disabled man, I am to look for those people, places, things, where God is hidden, and reveal Him. The best place, the best vantage point from which to do that is sitting at His feet, watching, listening, waiting, and then, writing. To a writer, that is obedience.

Sometimes I envision the Lord taking my chin in his hand and turning my head so I will see what He wants me to record. Sometimes I envision him touching my eyes so they can see. And finally, I take off my shoes. Finally, I worship the Giver instead of the gift. Finally I see the ripples of faith and truth slipping out across the pond of my life. And then I write.

Often God teaches me through "divine appointments." Often they happen when I think I am doing something mundane or even something that seems like drudgery. Like one day when I was working as a "rack jobber" (stocking book racks for a company called Living Books).

"Do you know anything about these flowers?" The young woman's eyes were hopeful, but I had to disappoint her and explain that I did not work in the hospital gift shop. I was just there to stock the book rack. I pointed to two ladies at a nearby counter. "Maybe they can help," I said.

She nodded, stared at the flower display and sighed. "I'm not really sure what I want."

I took note of her dress then—a baseball cap pulled over messy hair; a thin pair of pajama bottoms topped by a hospital issue housecoat wrapped around a frail frame; pull-on terrycloth slippers, two sizes too big.

"My friend is dying," she said, then turned back to me. "I am too."

I put my clipboard down and waited. Her story unfolded in simple language, the words slipping from her mouth almost as though rehearsed. She reached into a pocket and pulled out a picture of her seven-year-old daughter. I could see the resemblance. She smiled

159

when I mentioned it and went on to say there was a surgery that she was hoping for—highly experimental, there was only one doctor who could do it and he just happened to live in a nearby city. But then her voice fell and I had to lean close to hear. Her friend had had the surgery. She was still dying.

The conversation turned to the word hope then. She had hope they would agree to do the surgery, hope that, unlike her friend, she would recover, hope that she would live to watch her daughter grow up.

She said a pastor came to visit sometimes and "we say our small prayers together. They seem small, just words, but maybe not, eh?" Again that hopeful look in her eyes. I was praying small prayers right then. *She's so young, Lord. Please. Please.*

Then she was gone and I resumed stocking the rack. I did it once a month and in that hospital, the rack was usually almost empty by the time I returned. As I filled the pockets with books I was acutely aware of their contents. They hold pages about the love and mercy of Jesus, pages filled with stories of courage and faith, pages of humour to lift a sad heart and inspiration to encourage a weary soul. Pages of hope.

I knew I was sent there that day to do much more than just stock the book racks. My job suddenly seemed important. My other job, as a writer, suddenly seemed essential, "That I may publish with the voice of thanksgiving and tell of all thy wondrous works" (Psalm 26:7, KJV).

I realized it was essential, indeed, to declare the hope we have in Jesus Christ to those like that young woman who knew her time on this earth was coming to an end. Without such declarations of hope people are left bereft, in despair, and desperately alone. It is my task, as a writer of faith, to lead them to the One who can and will banish that despair so they know they are loved and forever held in his arms.

Chapter 18

Sometimes all you can do is stand back and watch God work as He makes the planets align.

That's how it felt on May 4th, 2015, my birthday, as I participated in the Budding Playwrights Festival at Rosebud School of the Arts in Rosebud, Alberta.

But let me go back a bit. Several years before I'd heard the Rosebud School of the Arts was running a playwriting course. I wanted to take it. Badly. But the course wasn't cheap and it would require a considerable chunk of time. I had neither, so I had to let the opportunity slip by.

When a friend sent me a link to the call for submissions for the course a couple of years later, I got excited again.

"Are you sure you'll have time for that?" My husband's words struck a cord. As a pastor's wife, my time and energies were often in demand; several writing deadlines loomed in my future, and I was booked for two speaking engagements. And then there was that book I wanted to finish.

As I read the syllabus and scanned the application for the course, I knew it would be demanding. The information came with a warning from the instructor: "If you aren't serious about doing the work, don't even begin." But I also knew I might not get another chance to do this—to be mentored by a playwright whose work

I knew and respected and to work with professional actors and directors.

So I prayed about it.

The ideas I'd had in the past, that always seemed to show up in my head as plays, began spinning feverishly, demanding to be let out. One in particular kept prodding—my father's war story about finding himself with the British soldiers who liberated Bergen-Belsen, the first concentration camp discovered as the war ended. I filled out the application, outlined the ideas I had, selected writing samples to send and updated my CV. When I hit send I had a definite sense of anticipation.

Once again doubts set in. Would I be accepted? I tried to prepare myself for a possible rejection but found I just couldn't imagine not doing this course. Receiving the email that told me I was in made me leap out of my chair. I couldn't wait to get started.

Then the work began—exercises geared to helping us choose a story, exercises geared to honing the skills necessary to make a play come alive on a stage, and the slow but tremendously exciting exercise of beginning to build a one act play. I found the process both challenging and exhilarating. It was pushing me and my writing to a new level. God had led me to a wonderful instructor, Lucia Frangione, author, playwright, teacher.

I remember the day I hit send and sighed. This first draft of the first act of my new play didn't come easily and I wasn't happy with what I'd produced. I knew there was something wrong but couldn't put my finger on what it was that left me wanting to drag the document into the trash. I thought about doing just that for the next few days as I watched my inbox with trepidation, believing my instructor's comments would not be encouraging. When her critique arrived I sighed again and hit the "open" button.

As usual, Lucia was frank about her thoughts and didn't hold back the criticism. But there were things she liked so I was encouraged. Then I got to the part that I knew wasn't right. And I started to smile. My instructor didn't mince words, but they were words I wanted to hear—words that clarified why the lines weren't working, words that made me want to jump right back in and get to work on it again. They were words that made me glad I hadn't dragged the document into the trash. And I was thankful.

The problem? My instructor expressed it this way:

It's your characters telling us what to make of that moment that begins to feel like the playwright 'telling us' what to think and feel, instead of trusting the moment and the image to speak for themselves. I like to think that I am called to plant the image, the debate, the relationship and I let the Holy Spirit do the rest. People love to figure things out for themselves. I think this is why Jesus spoke in obscure parables and resisted explaining right away. It's a holy practice—to ponder.

Yes! That was it exactly. I had simply gone too far, said too much, given too many answers instead of leaving the questions to be pondered. "A holy practice, to ponder." Yes. And another holy practice—to write sparingly, allowing the Holy Spirit room there, too.

Elie Wiesel once said: "Writing is not like painting where you add. It is not what you put on the canvas that the reader sees. Writing is more like a sculpture where you remove, you eliminate in order to make the work visible." The sculptor, Michaelangelo described the process this way: "I saw the angel in the marble and carved until I set him free. Every block of stone has a statue inside it, and it is the task of the sculptor to discover it."

It took some hard work and chipping away at my play, but after ten months an email arrived, saying, "Your play is ready. Congratulations."

I stared at the words and wept. *A Pattern in Blue* would be one of nine plays to be placed in the hands of a professional director and read on stage by professional actors.

I, of course, had no control over who was chosen to direct my play, nor the actors chosen for the three parts. I walked into the classroom where the rehearsal would take place and a middle-aged man introduced himself. He said he was excited about playing the parts of the doctor and the Rabbi. A younger man strolled in a minute later and I smiled. He was a perfect fit, physically, to play the part of my dad. The girl chosen to play the nurse seemed a bit young for the part, but then the director arrived, a man I recognized as the executive director of Rosebud!

As I sat there listening to them chat, I thought, *How could it get any better than this?* But then it did.

The director had taken the time to do some research on Bergen-Belsen, which he asked the actors to look at before they began the rehearsal so that everyone was "on the same page." Then he asked me several questions about the play and wanted to know where my dad had lived when he was a boy. When I told him he'd lived in a small town near Ottawa he asked the name of it. When I told him Perth, the young man who was to play my dad, almost spewed out his drink. "Wow," he said. "Are you kidding me? That's my hometown, where I was raised. All my family still lives there!"

Someone commented on the note in the script about a Jewish prayer that I had hoped could be read in Hebrew. I had added the English translation since I thought that was highly unlikely. The director turned to the man who would portray the Rabbi. He smiled and told us his family were in fact German Jews—and oh by the way, he was a Hebrew scholar and he had taken the time to write out the prayer in Hebrew and could chant it, as a Rabbi would, during the performance.

After four hours of watching the last rehearsal, during which the actors turned themselves into the characters in my play, it was time to go to the theatre. The director advised me to sit where I could scan the audience while the actors were on stage. The one act was almost halfway through before I remembered to do so. That's when the tears flowed again as I watched the rapt faces of that audience, caught up in the story, riveted by the good acting.

Later I told my husband, "I never have to celebrate another birthday. Nothing could ever beat this—what a gift!"

Writing that play about my father's experience during World War 2 was a journey of discovery. As I wrote his story, I learned about him—as a young man who stood, horrified, at the gates of Bergen-Belsen; as a husband who returned home broken and shaken to his core; as a father who remained an aloof stranger. And I learned about myself—as a teenager who got up in the night when I heard him making tea in the kitchen so I could have a conversation with him; as a young mother who fought my own emotional distance, and usually lost; as a Christian who had to find a way to forgive him for his aloofness and myself for responding to that in a way that did not honour him or God. As I wrote about my dad, God also showed me how to draw closer to Him and how to grow in the process of being more like Him.

Chapter 19

The process of writing is, in a way, a mysterious thing. The mystery lies in the fact that God is involved. He is doing something in me as I write.

The Jewish Talmud says, of craftsmen: "Their prayer is in the practice of their trade." Each time I take up the tools of my trade, I am in prayer. Each time I write, therefore, I would be wise to be listening.

I have heard it said that all art is autobiography, from the Greek, *autos* (self) + *bios* (life) + *graphein* (to write). I believe all art is also *deo*-biography. The art, the words that are in me, come not only from my experience of life, but from that inner core, from my spirit. Because Christ is resident there, and when I write from the depth of that place, I am, in a way, writing the life of Christ.

Maurice Blanchot has said. "To write is to make oneself the echo of what cannot cease speaking." I believe it is not a what, but a Who. I believe that because of the depth of His love for us, God cannot, will not, cease speaking to us. As I become an echo of Him, I realize He has given me my writing not only as a means to speak, but as a means to hear and understand.

I have three daughters who have taught and continue to teach me much. My eldest, Kate, is a wonderful young woman, whose path through adolescence had, as many do, a few rough spots. She was going through one of those times when she was asked to sing at our

167

church. She knew it was scheduled, she knew it was up to her to make all the arrangements.

When the Sunday morning came this is what happened. I fashioned it into a poem.

Singer

On our way to church, my daughter and I:
"Did you arrange for a pianist?"
"No."
"You're doing this a capella?"
"Yes."
"What song..."
"I don't know yet."
My voice, rising a decibel or two. Or maybe three:
"Then maybe you'd better postpone ..."
"No. I want to sing."
"But you should have arranged..."
"I know, Mother. But it will be fine. I just want to sing."
I sighed. Oh, my daughter.
Between Sunday School and the main service:
I found her in an empty classroom, her finger in a hymnal, her face turned toward the light of a far window. I opened my mouth, closed it again. Her eyes were open, but it felt like the room was full of prayer.
Later, in the sanctuary:
I watched her, sitting at the end of the pew, one long leg thrown over the other, the hymnal in her hand, finger still in it. She took a bulletin, scanned it, opened the hymnal, moved her finger to a different spot. I sighed, again.
They called on her, just before the sermon.
 On the podium:
She took the hymnal with her, left it closed, and sang: Jesu, Joy of Man's Desiring. And the room

168

filled with it, her voice, her face, her body yearning for it, drawing us up with her, up into the presence of our God. I held my breath.

Oh, my daughter.

And in the end:

I prayed forgiveness on myself, my need to work all things into my plan. I prayed release for all of us, to His will, His Spirit.

I wept. And then I smiled.

Oh, my daughter.

When that incident happened, I did not understand it. I did not know what it was I had learned. I only knew I had been deeply moved. Something in my spirit had responded to something in that song, and more, to the attitude in which it had been sung. Because I had been moved, I needed to express it, I needed to write it. As I began to write, I began to understand what it was God wanted to teach me.

When I am moved deeply, when I then attempt to express that moment, that experience, I believe I move toward wholeness, the wholeness that is in me because Christ is in me. And I learn more about Him. Prayer, in the practice of our trade.

There are many other stories of how God has taken me to that mysterious place, over the 30 plus years that I've been writing. The miracles abound but it has not always been easy. There have been times when it has seemed more like a chore than something I enjoyed doing. Times like the day I sat at my computer knowing my deadline was one hour away and the monitor screen was still blank.

It had been a busy week and I hadn't even started my column. Hadn't even thought about it. Hadn't even prayed. I typed the column heading and my name. I stopped. I clicked into my "ideas" file. Nothing inspired me. I went upstairs for a glass of water and decided my plants needed watering. I tidied up the living room. Half an hour later I went back to the computer. The screen was still blank. Finally, I prayed. Or rather, I whined. "Lord, I've been doing this for fifteen years. Maybe it's time I just quit." I was asking for permission.

What came to mind was a story a Bible translator told me in Papua New Guinea. He and his wife were working in a remote village. The translation work had not been going well. There had been many frustrations and he wondered if it really was worth the effort. Then he got dengue fever. Then they ran out of food and he had to almost literally crawl more than three and a half kilometers to the closest airstrip, only to discover the plane had been too full and hadn't brought their supplies. He decided he couldn't take any more. He went back to the village and told his national assistant he was quitting. He said the man nodded with compassion in his eyes, then said, "But you must understand, I cannot quit this work. It is what God wants me to do."

Those words were a rebuke to my missionary friend that day. The memory was a rebuke to me in that moment. I put my hands on the keyboard and started to type. I deleted most of what I wrote for the next three quarters of an hour, but then a sentence came. *Ah, yes, there it is*, I thought. Another followed and I had that assurance. *Yes. Go with that*. The column was a bit past deadline, and I thought it seemed a bit plain. But I copied and pasted it into an email and hit the send button.

The responses flooded back.

"You couldn't have known ..."

"This gave me the courage to change ..."

"Thank you for putting this into words that helped ..."

Some of them made me weep. All of them left me humbled by God's work and His presence with me as I wrote. Sometimes writing is a chore. But I cannot quit. It is what God wants me to do.

Yes, there have been frustrations galore—book signings where no one showed up (not one single soul!), royalties that took forever to get into my bank account and were much less than what I expected, and publishers that have to back out of agreements.

Although Larry Willard was excited about publishing the sequel to *One Smooth Stone*, when the economy took a sudden downturn, his company made the decision to drop all of their fiction line. That left me wondering how to get that second book published. I did not have the funds to self-publish. But God had a plan. My dear mother-in-law came to visit one day and asked when *A Tumbled Stone* was going to be released. When I explained that it was not going to happen, she said, "Well, we just can't have that!" She generously sponsored the publication of that book.

Then there are scheisters—those who prey on gullible writers desperate to see their words in print.

I was taken in by just such a person. I'll call him 'G.' Eventually I learned he had not given me his real name. I was invited to contribute to an anthology he was publishing. After weeks of back and forth editing of that story, he asked if I had any other manuscripts I'd like to see published. I told him about my fantasy series and he invited me to submit it. I was thrilled when he got back to me very quickly and said it had been accepted. The books were published and he put them onto Amazon.

I had been in touch with several other people, some Canadian, who were in his "stable" of writers and it wasn't long after the books appeared on Amazon that I began to hear grumblings from some of them. Then a woman who had published a series of romance novels with him let us all know that she had discovered 'G' was a fraud and was not paying any of his writers the royalties they were entitled to. She filed a lawsuit and won. When I began asking questions about my books I got only vague answers and promises of payments that never materialized. Eventually I demanded he take my books off of Amazon and I contacted that company to explain the situation. They told me there was little they could do since the books were controlled by his company, but in the end the books were removed. I saw no royalties from any of them.

But through it all God has continued to teach and encourage me to keep going. He has opened doors to teaching and speaking, sometimes in unexpected places, like a Legion organization that asked me to speak about Remembrance Day, and a Christian motorcycle group who filled a church to its limits to hear me talk about Jesus.

I almost said no to the second opportunity, until God made it clear that he wanted me to accept the invitation and let me know what I was to say. He even gave me the title, "The One Who Sticks Closer than a Brother." But I was more than a little nervous as I prepared that talk. The only bike I've ever been on was a mini trail bike when I was about eight years old. That's not much for "street cred" in the biker world. But then I thought about the message God had given me and realized how perfect it was for a group that prided itself on being a brotherhood. And I remembered what Jesus said to Moses in Exodus 4:12: "Now go; I will help you speak and will teach you what to say." Was it arrogant to expect He would do the same for me? The BOHO told me it was. But I remembered what happened when Moses asked Him to send someone else. God was angry. So I studied the scripture passage, and did what I was told.

It never ceases to amaze me when God shows up. That's what the message was about, and He demonstrated it that morning, when He showed up for those men and for me.

I'd had a number of writing projects on the go at that same time. I was using the precious days of summer to tie up some loose ends. One especially, that I almost let die. It was the fantasy series which almost published twice by reputable publishing houses, but each time the deals fell flat. That's when I ended up in the hands of that unscrupulous publisher and the second book never did make it to print, so I almost let the project die.

But I received an email from the mom of a boy who had read the first book. He was wondering about book two. Then someone else asked about it. I took that as an indication that God was saying, "Go." I pulled out those files and went to work, did some editing on book one, and refreshed my memory about Createspace, Amazon's publishing arm (now KDP). Book two was polished and I moved ahead to find a designer for the cover of book three. It was fun. I enjoyed renewing my acquaintance with the characters and playing with some of the plot line. Finding just the right images for the covers was also exciting.

I had no idea what God intended to do with those little books, but I knew He had said, "Go," and go I will. I'm pretty sure He's going to show up and demonstrate His sovereignty once again, even when it concerns a fantasy series that I thought was dead.

He's like that. And when He says "Go," I've come to understand it's best not to argue.

Chapter 20

But sometimes God gives me a faithful "no." As on the day when, looking for ways to sell more books, I clicked into a local church's website to see if there were any events coming up. I was hoping they might allow me to set up a book table. I was glad to see there was an event very soon, so I e-mailed the woman in charge with my idea.

She e-mailed back, but the answer was no. The committee thought it might be too much of a distraction. That did not brighten my mood. Other doors had closed that week and, as I looked at the total number of books I had managed to sell in the past year, I became discouraged. I sat at my computer that day and thought, once again, maybe I should just quit.

But I went to the event. It was a live video feed with a well-known speaker. As I walked into the sanctuary that Friday evening, I wasn't feeling in the mood—I was still angry and frustrated and, underneath, wondered why God wasn't helping me to get the word out about my books.

The video began and I found it did nothing to help. The sound was a bit wobbly and the music seemed "canned." I thought, oh yeah, here we go with another hyped-up "performance" that will leave me cold.

Then the speaker began. Slowly her passion and sincerity broke through. Her humour lifted the heaviness. And I began to listen for what God was saying to me. He said plenty. Then the worship group came back on and suddenly the music lifted me into that place of praise and worship. By the end of the evening I was in tears at God's wonderful grace and mercy and unconditional love. I felt ashamed at my lack of trust.

The next day was more of the same. I don't think it was a coincidence that the message was from Luke 8, which lays out the parable of the sower and talks about those who hear but don't respond, those who in "the time of testing fall away," and those who "hear, but as they go on their way they are choked by life's worries, riches and pleasures and they do not mature." I realized I could put myself in all those categories and asked for forgiveness.

I left that place with a renewed sense of how alive my God is, how good, and how faithful. Best of all, I had a renewed passion for His Word—something that had been lacking in my life for a while. And I was so glad for that faithful "no." Had I been concerned with selling books I would have been distracted from what God wanted to say to me. I might not have heard Him at all.

He was telling me I needed to be attentive to His word, to His voice, to His will. I needed to recognize the times when He says "no" aren't meant to punish me, as the BOHO would have me believe, but times when He has something important that I need to hear before I can truly do the work He has called me to do. I need to receive His "No" in order to hear His "Go."

I am often asked where my ideas come from. That's a hard question to answer because they come from a variety of sources, often from things I see God do right before my eyes. Like on this day, when He showed me one of those "common bushes afire with God" that Elizabeth Barrett Browning's poem describes.

The day was bright and sunny with just a touch of crispness to it. It was the kind of morning that should have lifted my spirits, but as I gazed out the window my thoughts were far away and all gloomy. I sighed and tried to prepare for the day ahead. I knew it wasn't going to be an easy one.

There would be the gathering of friends and family at the church and then the funeral and a reception immediately afterward. My friend's death had been a shock to us all. As I got ready I prayed that the Lord would help me get through the day.

I heard the birds as I was eating breakfast. At first I didn't pay much attention. There was a large tract of bush on the other side of our street, so we heard the birds every morning. But by the time I was ready to head out our front door, I was wondering why the birdsong was so loud. As I stepped out into the fresh spring air, I was astonished at the reason. The entire bush, every branch on every tree across from me was full of robins. They flitted from branch to branch and tree to tree, singing. I stood and watched and listened and my spirit was lifted. A verse of scripture that can sometimes seem so impossible came to mind. "My grace is sufficient for you" (2 Corinthians 12:9). I was witnessing an act of grace, a gift given in reply to a plea for help. The gift worked wonders.

I don't know if robins usually move about in large flocks. Perhaps it's part of their migration pattern, but I had never seen a flock like that before, or since. Like many people I've always looked for that single robin that heralds the coming of spring. I would never have dreamed of looking for a flock of hundreds.

Perhaps God knew that's what I needed that day— something unusual and delightful, something that would take my breath away. As I drove to the church I realized that it's just like Him to do something like that. He has said that He does not only want to give us life, but He wants to give us abundant life (John 10:10), a life full of delightful things like birdsong, to banish the gloom, a life in which the darkness of death is overcome by the blazing light of life. I consider it a privilege to be able to write about such things, as He reveals them to me.

And then there was this day:

The day had been grey, a fine drizzle of rain creating a thickening mist that shifted and swallowed all in its path. My husband and I were to drive to the high point on The Dome behind Dawson City, Yukon, the next morning, and I prayed the morning sun would banish the fog and let us see the stunning view of the Klondike Valley. I hadn't seen it for many years, and I longed for the exhilaration it had always given me. But the next morning the fog lingered.

"Let's go up anyway," my husband said, "at least as far as the cemetery." I knew what he intended. The cemetery held the graves of our two close friends, the men in their twenties who had taken their own lives in a suicide pact many years before. Their deaths had been the catalyst for our journey to faith in Jesus. We wandered among the graves, noting names we recognized from years gone by. How young some of them had been when death claimed their mortal bodies.

We found the graves we were looking for—one marked by the idler wheel of a D6 Cat, the other by the front frame of a piece of heavy machinery. Fitting for two men involved in gold mining. I watched as my husband pushed scrub brush away so we could see their names welded on the unusual headstones. Memories of that time brought a somber stillness to the place.

Neither of us wanted to head back down into town, so we continued up the dirt road as it wound its way to the top. The peak of The Dome was above the clouds so we looked down on the grey shifting mist, watching as it slowly began to dissipate. A small patch of blue appeared. Part of the Yukon River. I was puzzled when I saw it emerge. At this point in the river's course, the Yukon is not blue. It's a milky grey, filled with silt from two rivers upstream. Then I realized the river was reflecting the blue sky above, slowly being revealed as the clouds moved away.

I thought of all the people who had come into our lives at that time of death and tragedy, people who prayed with us and guided us toward the truth about life, death and eternity. And I smiled. They themselves were just ordinary people, living ordinary lives in an isolated place, but they reflected something from beyond themselves. Something that glowed with the colour of vibrancy and life—the face of God Himself.

I pray that will be the case with everything I write. Though it may have little that is called extraordinary in its pages, though it may exist in a world filled with shifting fog, may it be a reflection of truth, flowing with the colour of true life, able to translate into healing, able to reflect the love of a holy God. May it draw my readers along, as that small patch of blue river below us did, to a place where they will meet Him and know Him, just a little bit more than they did before.

Chapter 21

Ideas also often come from conversations I've had with friends and family. My latest book, *Merrigold's Very Best Home*, came from a conversation with my middle daughter, Laura.

Laura has always leaned toward minimalism. But when she came home after working as a missionary in Bangladesh she was an all out flaming minimalist. Years later, I was visiting her and my two grandkids one day when she expressed how difficult it was to maintain that philosophy now that she had children: "I don't want my kids to grow up believing they're entitled to all the things the advertising world hawks. I want them to be grateful for what they have, not always wanting more, not always needing to have the latest fad."

At some point during that conversation the focus shifted to some of the antics she and her sisters had gotten up to when they were kids. We laughed at one such incident, when Katie, my oldest daughter, decided to run away from home. At the age of five she had gotten a bit upset with me for something and decided she should find another place to live. She packed a little suitcase and headed off to her best friend's house, one block away. I called her best friend's mom to let her know she was about to have a visitor. Kate didn't stay long and we sorted things out when she got home.

As I drove home that evening I thought about that story and about Laura's minimalist dilemma. I wondered if somehow I could combine the two things into a children's story. I started to play "what if" and the story evolved of a little girl who runs away from home and visits a few animal friends who invite her to stay in their houses. She discovers that none of their homes are suitable for her and eventually returns to her own home where she is welcomed and loved by her parents.

It did not take long to put that story on paper when I got home. I wasn't sure what to do with it, so I sent it to a friend, Colleen McCubbin, who had started up a small boutique publishing company, Siretona Creative. Colleen loved the story and urged me to consider publishing it.

We began discussing options and I discovered that publishing a children's book is quite expensive, mostly due to the cost of hiring an illustrator. Colleen suggested I try doing a crowdfunding event to help fund the project. I was more than hesitant.

The BOHO was laughing. "You really think people will support it, support you?" I wondered, *What if no one does? Could I handle that kind of rejection? And where would I find an illustrator?* This was an entirely new learning curve for me and I realized it was going to take a lot of prayer to make it come about.

I was attending a women's Bible study group at the time and decided to test the waters by asking them to pray that God would lead me to the right person to illustrate *Merrigold's Very Best Home*. When the Bible study ended a woman approached me and said I should talk to the woman who taught the group. "Her daughter went to university with a young woman who illustrates books." Within the week I had been connected to Kyla Wiebe. When I looked at her portfolio online I knew God had led me directly to the right person for the job.

After more prayer and encouragement from Colleen, I decided to risk it and set up an Indiegogo campaign with a goal of reaching $2,000 to pay for Kyla's artwork.

I was stunned when I reached the half-way point within the first few days. In the end the campaign exceeded the goal. I hired Kyla and was delighted when she was open to using my granddaughter Thea as the model for Merrigold, and my own Berne-doodle, Livy, as a model for the dog. The process to see the book in print took a few months as Kyla sent me sketches and we settled on the changes I wanted. Colleen handled all the publishing details and it was not long before I held a copy of *Merrigold's Very Best Home* in my hands. It has been a delight to receive pictures and even a video or two of kids reading and enjoying the Merrigold book.

When I look back on those days, I realize my fear of raising funds through a crowdfunding campaign ran deep. I remembered the time when I had just spoken to a group of Christian women. The response had been wonderful, God's presence evident. It was thrilling and humbling to know He had used my words, once again, to draw women closer to Himself.

One of those women approached and asked which of my books I would recommend. We moved to the book table and chatted. She chose a devotional book and asked me to sign it. When she moved away, one of the leaders of the organization approached. I could tell she was not pleased. She explained that she'd been talking with another author who had applied to be a speaker for the group. "She told me someone had told her that our group was a good place to sell books." Her eyebrows arched. I knew she knew that "someone" was me. I was puzzled as to why the woman was upset until she said, "We're in the business of bringing people to Christ, not selling books!" She marched off in a huff before I could respond.

I pondered her words, and my motives, as I drove home. Was I wrong to sell my books at these venues? I prayed about it and when I received an email from someone telling me how one of my books had helped her, I realized God had answered.

I realized, too, the leader of that group failed to see my books as an extension of the ministry God had given me. This wasn't a new experience. Even mentioning my books in a church sometimes met with disapproval. But I have seen how God has worked through the words in my writing.

Perhaps such negative reaction from some Christians lurked in my subconscious when I contemplated launching that fundraising campaign. Negative thoughts niggled. Wasn't there something wrong with asking for money to do this? When two sizable donations arrived one morning, that niggle of guilt increased. Who was I to ask people to give me money?

I don't think it was a coincidence that the email I received from Scripture Union Canada that same morning dealt with 1 Chronicles 29:1–20. For several days previous, I'd been following the story of David's desire to build the temple in Jerusalem and was struck again by God's provision. I found myself wishing I'd been there in those days, so that I too could give toward the building project David initiated and tasked his son Solomon to complete. On that particular morning, the words of the scripture struck me in a different way. David lists all that he has given to the project, then addresses the leaders of Israel and asks, "Now, who is willing to consecrate themselves to the Lord today?" (1 Chronicles 29:5b, NIV). The next two verses hit me:

Then the leaders of families, the officers of the tribes of Israel, the commanders of thousands and commanders of hundreds, and the officials in charge

184

of the king's work gave willingly. They gave toward the work on the temple of God ...

David asked the people to give because it was the Lord's project, a part of the building of God's kingdom on earth. They responded generously and with joy because they too realized it was a privilege to be able to do so.

David goes on in verse 14, "But who am I, and who are my people, that we should be able to give as generously as this? Everything comes from you, and we have given you only what comes from your hand. ... And now I have seen with joy how willingly your people who are here have given to you."

I do not suggest that my tiny children's book project is in any way comparable to the building of the temple in Jerusalem. But I know that it is a tiny thing that is God-ordained. It has been obvious that it was His will that this book, and indeed, all of my books, be completed, and I believe it was His will that others were given the opportunity to contribute to it. It may be a very tiny pebble in the grand scheme of the building of His kingdom, but God seems to think it needs to be there. It may even cause a few ripples across many ponds that will go on and on and on.

And so I pray with David, "Lord, ... keep these desires and thoughts in the hearts of your people forever, and keep their hearts loyal to you" (1 Chronicles 29:18, NIV). I pray that we, as writers of faith, might continue to build His kingdom together, one tiny pebble at a time.

Once again, God showed me that He had a plan. All I had to do was be faithful and committed to seeing it through.

A poet named Don Marquis once wrote, "Publishing a volume of verse is like dropping a rose petal down the Grand Canyon and waiting for the echo." These days, you could substitute the word "book" for the phrase "volume of verse." The quote makes me think of a cartoon I saw once and wish I had copied. It's of a writer sitting at a desk surrounded by thousands of volumes in a library. An eager fan holds out a copy of his book for him to sign. The caption reads, "Being a writer must make you feel so … so significant!"

The puzzled look on the writer's face made me laugh out loud. I know how he feels, and if you are a writer, I'm sure you do too. Imposter syndrome lurks and springs to life at the least indication of inadequacy, real or imagined.

In the face of the plethora of written work I sometimes wonder why on earth I am driven to write. Hasn't it all been said? Haven't better writers already captured my thoughts on the page? Many will say the answer is no, but sometimes it's hard to believe it. That's when I need to give my head a shake and realize that I am wrestling "against the spiritual forces of evil in the heavenly places" (Ephesians 6:12, ESV). That's when I need to call my prayer team. That's when I need to turn to friends who understand and are there, ready to support me in the battle.

I have learned that only then will I believe and accept the truth. My thoughts, said in my voice, have not been heard and yes, they are significant. They are significant not just because I have done my apprenticeship and reached a level of skill and expertise, but because God wants to use them. I am His child, unique in the universe. He has a purpose for my life—for the whole of it, including the words in my mind and heart, those unique words that I put into a computer and send out to a publisher. The expression of that uniqueness, when done with pure motive, honours my Creator. The denial of it denies His grace and mercy. Therefore, it is not only fitting that I do it, it is commanded.

1 Peter 4:10 says, "Each one should use whatever gift he has received to serve others, faithfully administering

God's grace in its various forms." That tells me that what I write is a form of God's grace to be extended to others, no matter how insignificant I feel, no matter how small the audience may be, no matter the state of the economy or world affairs.

Don Marquis' quote could leave me with a sense of futility unless I know there is an echo, even the infinitely small sound of a rose petal falling in the Grand Canyon. The smallest of echoes has meaning when it is an echo of my Creator's purpose. So, as a writer of faith, I toss my rose petals to the winds, scatter them with prayer and thanksgiving. I believe they are significant in God's economy. They may even change a life.

I thought about this one day when I wandered by a pond near our home on what I thought might be the last day in which to enjoy a beautiful autumn. The sun was still high, making the trees glow as they shivered in a cool breeze. A single yellow leaf floated down from a poplar tree leaning out over the pond. Landing on the still water, it created a slight ripple. It was more like a tremor, really, that shimmered and radiated out across the pond in a wide ring. Such a small thing, I thought, yet it created a still moment, a focus of beauty that I attempted to catch with my camera, a still moment in time that triggered thoughts which carried me on for the rest of the afternoon.

Later that day I came across something the great artist Vincent Van Gogh apparently said in a letter to his brother: "Great things are not done by impulse, but by a series of small things brought together."

I try to remember those words when I feel that my writing career, my body of work, has been too small to have any effect at all. And I remember what Mother Teresa once said, "We can do no great things; only small things with great love."

Jesus continually asked His disciples to do small things: "Let down the nets for a catch," He said and

His sovereignty over all things was revealed. (Luke 5:4) "Take and eat ... Drink," He urged them and they learned what dying to self was all about (Matthew 26:26-27). "Give them something to eat," He commanded and showed them a generosity of provision that was astonishing (Matthew 14:16). "Wash in the pool," He directed and revealed the depth of His compassion (John 9:7). Such small, ordinary actions. Such wide-reaching ripples when they were obeyed and executed in love.

God has placed me in a small pond. Has He given me seemingly insignificant things to do, to say, to write? But then I remember His words to the prophet Zechariah: "Do not despise these small beginnings, for the Lord rejoices to see the work begin" (Zechariah 4:10, NLT).

Small things done in obedience, in love, leaving tremors that may very well create ripples that will never end. Like a yellow leaf landing on still water. Recently I spoke with a retired man who looked back on a long career. He mentioned the fact that he was often sent to far away and rather desolate places where he despaired of ever being able to 'climb the corporate ladder.' Then a colleague said something that changed his attitude. "Think of it this way. If you climbed that ladder you'd end up being a very small fish in a very big pond. This way, you're a pretty big fish in a very small pond. Where do you think you'll have the most influence?"

Looking back on my writing career, I realize the wisdom in those words.

There is so much that etches a thin line around my tiny speck of faith, so much that I see "through a glass, darkly" (1 Corinthians 13:12, KJV). But then there are moments, like a while ago, when I sat with a cup of good coffee in front of a comforting fireplace and watched as a tiny girl dressed in a red snowsuit skated an elegant loop around the pond across the street. And I am so thankful for all the "common bushes," all the small graces, the atoms of hope that form and design my days like the multitude of pixels in a digital photograph.

All I need is that simple faith, the smallest drop of faith, as the scripture says, even as much as the size of a mustard seed.

Jesus compared His kingdom to that mustard seed as He wandered the roads and byways of Jerusalem and beyond. He said, "It is like a mustard seed, which a man took and planted in his garden. It grew and became a tree, and the birds perched in its branches" (Luke 13:19, NIV).

When I read this passage, I noticed the parts to this little story. The man took the seed—he was willing to receive something from God. Then he planted it—he took action and used what God had given him. As a result, the plant grew into what God had intended it to be. And finally, the birds came and made it their own—the plant was useful and appreciated.

I love that last phrase—it's one of those atoms of hope for me because it speaks of purpose and usefulness and blessing. That tiny seed buried in the earth resulted in a flourishing plant, part of a beautiful garden that brought joy and peace to those around it. That gives me hope for the tiny seeds I have spread and planted in my lifetime. I may not even be aware of most of them, but God can use them to bring about His purposes.

It is of use to ask myself what steps I need to take to make myself open to receive these small graces? What will it take for me to be one who sees and takes off my shoes, as Elizabeth Barrett Browning encourages us to do?

Chapter 22

It's funny how your brain integrates things into your dreams.

It began with a birthday card. My friend Pauline is usually the first to send me a card as the day approaches, likely because her day is not long behind mine. I received her card this year with mixed emotions, though it did give me a chuckle. Her cards are always funny. This particular birthday wasn't a "milestone" as such, though it did make me ponder a bit more than some had, for some reason. It seemed inconceivable that so many years had passed by. As my friend Pauline said, "How the heck did that happen?"

Then I had this dream. It's unusual for me to remember my dreams, but this one remained clear and vivid. As I pondered it over my morning coffee, I realized it included a few not-so-subtle metaphors for my life at the time.

The setting of the dream was Dawson City, Yukon, where Pauline and I had met way back in the early '70s. In the dream, a big storm blew down the top part of a large tree in the backyard of Pauline's house. It had not touched the house but left a lot of debris in the yard. This was the second tree that had blown down. The first one, a limbless though still tall stump, stood in the opposite corner of the yard.

Pauline was trying to cut the fallen limbs into sections with a Swede saw. I told her I knew someone who would do it with a chainsaw, a much more efficient tool for the job. (I had once tried to cut a huge woodpile into manageable chunks with a Swede saw, so I knew whereof I spoke.) Pauline agreed and we called him over. The man in the dream has also been a friend and writing mentor of sorts, for some time, but in this scenario, he owned a beauty salon next door. Yup—a writer/hairdresser with a chain saw! This was one of those rather surreal dreams. My friend came over and made short work of cutting the remaining branches off the tree and clearing the yard.

Then he suggested we do something with all the wood. Yes, the tree was old and had fallen down, but the wood was still useful, he reasoned. The decision was made to build an addition onto Pauline's house with the wood from the tree, using the two tall stumps as corner posts. The walls went up quite quickly. Then my chainsaw wielding friend took one of the branches, sawed it into a small plank and engraved the word "Legacy" on it.

There are a few things about this dream that made me go, "Huh!"

The fallen trees—my husband had recently announced his intention to retire as pastor of the church we had planted fifteen years before. The trees were birch trees—you know, the kind with the white bark that you can peel and write on. I think they also represent my writing career. It has made me realize that my life, and my career, in some ways, are winding down, being trimmed down to bare essentials, but "the wood" that remains is still useful.

The addition on the house—our church was approaching the point of not only looking for a new pastor, but eventually building or finding a new place to call home. We started it in 2005 and had almost outgrown the building we'd purchased. I'd like to think this also represents my writing career, as I continue to move into teaching others who are coming after, building new things.

And that word, legacy—oh my. I've been thinking a lot about what I have and haven't accomplished over the past number of years of my life. Will I leave anything at all behind that is of value, besides a closet full of unsold books? I hope so. Putting this book together has walked me through some of the highlights, things God has used from my life that have been fodder for my writing, things that have made a difference. It has been a joyful process and a humbling one. It fills me with awe to look back on it now and see what God has done.

I love the book of 1 Samuel. Especially this verse: "The Lord was with Samuel as he grew up, and he let none of Samuel's words fall to the ground" (1 Samuel 3:19, NIV).

I took great encouragement from this verse when it arrived in my inbox one day. The calling of Samuel has always held a fascination for me. There are many things to be gleaned from that passage of scripture, many that pertain to being a writer.

Samuel responded to the call even though he was not sure what it was, where it was coming from or where it would lead. Sometimes the nudges I get from the Lord are like that. I'm not sure about them, but I move forward in faith. Sometimes I feel God is telling me to write a certain article or poem or book. I have no way of knowing what God intends for that piece of writing but I show it to friends, have it critiqued, finally submit it, and perhaps see it published. Then I stand back in awe at the amazing things God does with it.

Samuel sought out the wisdom of his mentor and it was Eli who directed him to turn to the Lord and to respond. My mentors, encouragers, prayer warriors and critique partners are all vital in my growth as a Christian writer. They have been put in my life for good reason. I need to seek their counsel and help often. I need to heed the advice and critiques of my work, recognize others see weaknesses that I am blind to, and be willing to make the changes necessary.

Samuel stayed close to the Lord throughout his life and became one of the great prophets of Israel. He learned obedience at Eli's knee and never forgot it. Note the last phrase in the scripture above: "and he let none of Samuel's words fall to the ground." All of what Samuel spoke to the people of Israel bore fruit for God. Nothing was wasted.

It is the Lord who directs and guards my words. It is the Lord who will take them to the right people at the right time and use them for His purposes. Note the word, "none." I take great encouragement from that word alone. Nothing God pours through me is wasted. Each article, each poem, each novel, each devotional, each book will bear the fruit He has in mind. Even those things I write that may never appear in print are important as part of the process. They are doing things in me, and the results will show in my work. I may not always see the results God has intended, but I can be assured that they will be accomplished.

In God's economy, nothing is wasted. Not even one word. And so, I leave you now with these words:

Concerning all acts of initiative there is one elemental truth, the ignorance of which kills countless ideas and splendid plans: that moment one definitely commits oneself, then Providence moves too. All sorts of things occur to help that would never have otherwise occurred. A whole stream of events issues from the decision, raising in one's favor all manner of unforeseen incidents, meetings, and material assistance which no man or woman would have dreamed could have come his way. Whatever you can do, or dream you can do, begin it. Boldness has genius, power, and magic to it. Begin it now.

- Johann Wolfgang von Goethe

If you believe God has called you to write for the building of His kingdom on this earth, take that step of obedience. Silence your BOHO by doing what the Bible tells us to do: "take every thought captive to obey Christ" (2 Corinthians 10:5, ESV).

My battle with the Big Old Hairy Ogre is still ongoing, but in a way that's a good thing, because when I find myself listening to him it wakes me up to the fact that I haven't turned my eyes upon the One who guides and encourages me onto the path I am meant to follow. It's then I know what I must do—"seek first the kingdom of God and his righteousness" (Matthew 6:33), and trust in the truth of Isaiah 41:13—"For I am the LORD your God who takes hold of your right hand and says to you, do not fear; I will help you."

What if?

What if Abram didn't pull up the tent pegs and
set off from Ur?

What if Noah didn't pick up the hammer?

What if Moses didn't pick up the staff?

What if Gideon didn't climb out of the winepress
and break down the altar to Baal?

What if Joshua didn't march around Jericho?

What if Ruth didn't go with Naomi?

What if David didn't take the provisions to his
brothers on the front lines?

What if Solomon didn't build the temple?

What if Shaphan the secretary didn't read the
book of the Law to Josiah?

What if Josiah didn't tear his robes?

What if Esther stayed home?

What if Daniel didn't pay attention to his dreams?

What if Matthew didn't walk away from the tax
collector's booth?

What if Peter didn't put down his nets?

What if you don't take up your pen?

Acknowledgements

This book would never have become a reality without the help of the wonderful team at Siretona Creative, Colleen McCubbin and Celeste Ferguson in particular.

It was Colleen who urged me to expand on the interview I did with Marg Gibb in 2023. "You have to write a memoir!" Colleen said. That seed took root, and this book is the result.

Then Celeste's careful eye for the big picture helped me to see the weaknesses in the manuscript.

Susan Plett also graciously gave me some advice that was invaluable as we worked on the final draft, and Ashley Mitchell added helpful line editing.

My writer families, who have been wonderfully supportive, are owed a debt I can never repay. Thanks to InScribe Christian Writer's Fellowship, Foothills Writers Group, The Scribblies, the Narrow Road Writers, and The Word Guild. Bless you all for believing in me and my work.

I also want to thank my husband Spencer who has put up with living in the same house with a slightly obsessed writer. His support has been ongoing and his urging to put down my laptop now and then has no doubt kept me from becoming totally sedentary and detached from the world. Thank you, my love!

I also want to thank my daughter, Meagan, for the great photo on the back cover, and my other two—Kate and Laura—for letting me tell stories about them, even when I forget to ask if it's okay!

My husband Spencer and I in 2015

photo by Jasmine McLean

With my dog, Klondike, on the top of the Dome behind Dawson City

Wearing the parka I made, Bear Creek, 1978

Spencer and I enjoying a "moo-moo bundle" in Ukarumpa, Papua New Guinea

I am holding a 'bilum' gifted to me by friends Iya & Mifao in Ukarumpa, Papua New Guinea

At work in the Non-Print Media Department, Ukarumpa, Papua New Guinea

Signing books at a women's retreat in Saskatchewan

With Violet Nesdoly, launching our books at the InScribe
Conference 2007

Speaking to a Christian Women's Club in Alberta

More books by Marcia

www.marcialeelaycock.com